PAID TO $PEAK!

HOW TO BECOME A PROFESSIONAL SPEAKER

DR. KEVIN C. SNYDER

This book is the product of 20 years of experience – some pleasure and some pain. I have documented everything I know about becoming a PAID professional speaker and I am confident you learn new techniques and strategies that will result in PAID speaking opportunities.

I have read numerous other books on professional speaking and found significant gaps in what they share, and more importantly, what they don't share. Most do not provide a fraction of the business strategy that PAID speaking requires, nor do they provide the templates and personal examples that I'll be sharing with you in this book. PAID speaking is a business, as you'll soon read.

While reading this book, and afterwards, I would be honored to hear from you. Feel free to drop me a question or comment at my personal email – Kevin@KevinCSnyder.com. After you complete the book, I will also be happy to provide you with a complimentary 30-minute coaching call to review your speaking materials and answer any questions you may have about the book.

I'd also appreciate your feedback by writing a **customer review on Amazon**. In appreciation for leaving a review, here's how:

Simply follow these steps below:

#**1**: In the Amazon.com search bar, type "How to Become a Professional Speaker and Kevin Snyder" so that you find the book online. Then click on the book title!

#**2**: Scroll down where it states "Write a Customer Review." Click that button. You will write your review there.

Note: Although Amazon.com preferred, you can also visit my website to make book reviews/purchases or contact me directly for bulk discount orders. (www.KevinCSnyder.com Kevin@KevinCSnyder.com)

Copyright © by Kevin C. Snyder

All rights reserved. No part of this publication may be used or reproduced, stored in a retrieval system, or transferred in any form by any means, except in brief quotations in a review, without the express written consent of the individual author/editor. All quotes contained within this book are written by the author unless credit is specifically given to another source.

How To Become a Professional Speaker: PAID To SPEAK!™ is a registered trademark and cannot be used or copied without permission.

ISBN-13: 978-1505436266

Library of Congress Cataloging-in-Publication Data:
Snyder, Kevin C.
    How To Become a Professional Speaker: PAID To $PEAK!™

Edited by Write Way Publishing Company
Layout and Design by Write Way Publishing Company
www.WriteWayPublishingCompany.com

For additional information:
Dr. Kevin C. Snyder
www.KevinCSnyder.com

Follow Kevin on your social of choice
@KevinCSnyder

Download Kevin's *app* on your phone/iPad to get your "Daily Dose" of motivation, access to contact Kevin directly, leadership resources ... & much more! Simply go to your app store and find **KevinCSnyder**

Book Reviews

Darryl B., Charlotte, NC

I highly recommend "How to Become a Professional Speaker: Paid to Speak!" to anyone looking to get into the speaking business. I had the pleasure of attending Kevin's workshop/seminar in Raleigh, North Carolina where I received this book while he walked us through the content. Since the workshop, I have read the book through two times and STILL haven't caught all the value that's in here. Here's some of the Gold in the book:

-Action steps at the end of each Module (This is not just fluff, this book has actual steps to get you through the process)

-Speaking Storyboard (I used this to outline for my last Toastmaster Speech and received Best Speech that day)

-Personal Stories which give you an inside look on Kevin's story and the speaking Industry

-Examples of sample emails, contracts, etc. available in the book and upon request (worth the price of the book 50x)

-Free 30 minute coaching session after reading the book.

Randy F., Scottsdale, AZ

This is a fabulous step-by-step book for not only emerging and aspiring professional speakers, but also for professional speakers themselves. Dr. Snyder provides so many excellent nuggets of wisdom in this book that it is impossible not to benefit greatly from whatever phase of professional speaking you are at currently. I'm a beginning speaker and this book has already helped me tremendously in providing clarity on where to begin! What I like most about this book is how his chapters are designed as coaching modules. With reflective questions throughout and a chapter summary and checklist, this book is really designed as a workbook so you can immediately apply the concepts being presented. You should read with a pen and expect to work as you read! This is extremely helpful and the only book like it of its kind.

Joe N., Raleigh, NC

"How to Become a Professional Speaker" is a great resource for both brand new speakers as well as professional speakers that find what has been working in the past just isn't working anymore. Kevin made this an easy to follow resource with many opportunities to reflect on why we want to be in the business, why we stay in the business and where do we want to go.

The second chapter in the book is titled "Where to Start." It doesn't get any easier than that. The problem with most Do-it-Yourself books is that it is never clear as to where you should start. This book is different. The rest of the book is a roadmap, with a specific route outlined straight to success. Once again, thank you Kevin Snyder for writing this book.

Shannon F., Durham, NC

I honestly loved this book! This is a clearly defined step by step guide on how to accomplish exactly what the book's title suggests: "How to get paid to speak!" I've seen courses, seminars, webinars and coaching programs up to several thousand dollars and Dr. Snyder is offering to his readers at a fabulous price. In full disclosure, I actually didn't follow Dr. Snyder's advice in the book to the tee. He purposefully instructs the reader to accomplish each task before moving on to the next chapter. I actually consumed the book in one weekend absolutely devouring the text. I had a journal next to me and took diligent notes, as well. I then scheduled time on my calendar for each chapter so that I would not be distracted.

Matt B., Maine

If you desire to become a speaker, then you need to read this book. Even if you currently speak but want more results, this book will provide you with incredible content and recommendations for improving your speaking business. When the book arrived, I was pleased to find that it was in workbook form and had excellent reflective questions that guided me alongside the content. This style is exactly what I needed. Don't TELL me what to do, SHOW me. Dr. Snyder did just that in this book ... it's excellent. Read it and apply it!

Travis M., Texas

Outstanding book! I've read several others but this book is the most helpful and practical with guided steps. Not only is the author transparent in his writing style but he's also dedicated to the process of helping others identify their plan to become a speaker. I love the personal examples that Kevin shares in this book. I have already re-read the book twice and am absorbing more even the 2nd time ... highly recommended for anyone who desires to be a speaker!

Pete H., Orlando, FL

This is a fabulous step-by-step book for not only emerging and aspiring professional speakers, but also for professional speakers themselves. Dr. Snyder provides so many excellent nuggets of wisdom in this book that it is impossible not to benefit greatly from whatever phase of professional speaking you are at currently. I'm a beginning speaker and this book has already helped me tremendously in providing clarity on where to begin!

Dr. Snyder is 110% transparent in this book. You'll read about his good fortunes but also about many of his mistakes. You'll laugh and you'll also gasp in awe at some of the amazing experiences he has had both on and off stage, during travels, and through the contractual process of getting paid speaking bookings. I appreciated his writing style, his candor, and his uplifting - and sometimes direct - tone. He writes as he speaks and that makes him, and also this book, very relatable. I see why he's an excellent speaker.

Overall, a great read and something I will need to re-read again and again to ensure I am applying these wonderful concepts!

About The Author

Dr. Kevin Snyder is a professional speaker and author with a passion for helping individuals find and live theirs.

He has spoken for over 500,000 people through 1,150 presentations in all 50 states and numerous countries. His keynote audiences range from high schools & colleges to corporate organizations and associations of all types.

Before becoming a professional speaker, Kevin served as Dean of Students for High Point University in High Point, North Carolina and has worked in Student Affairs for institutions including University of South Carolina, University of Central Florida, and Embry-Riddle Aeronautical University. Kevin earned his Doctorate in Educational Leadership from the University of Central Florida and focused his dissertation research on retention factors for first-generation college students.

 Kevin is also the Senior Publishing Consultant at Write Way Publishing Company, a self-publishing company he founded to help other aspiring authors become published.

Kevin is also a columnist for several magazines, a certified skydiver, scuba diver, sailing enthusiast and a former game show winner on ... **'The Price Is Right!'
Come on Down!**

Dedication

To Michael, you didn't know it at the time, but you gave me my first paid gig - $250.

To Karen, on that cold day in Chicago, you shared your story and helped me realize that speaking is about sharing a message that connects to others.

This book is also dedicated to YOU, the reader, for being a future agent of change through speaking and by sharing your story. You'll be inspiring people, sharing your expertise, and making this world a better place. Kudos to you.

Contents

Introduction

Author Preface

Module 1: Where to Start
- Setting your foundation
- Importance of an abundance mindset
- Dissecting an incredible speech
- Answering the three most important questions
- Preparing for the most common question you will receive

Module 2: Developing Your Program
- Breaking through speaking mythbusters
- Understanding what you need to get booked
- Developing your One Page
- Designing your presentation
- Identifying practice opportunities

Module 3: Finding Opportunities & Getting Found
- Finding speaking engagements
- Crafting the best outreach
- Speaking to colleges and universities
- Getting referrals and inquiries
- Sharing content to brand yourself

Module 4: Getting PAID to SPEAK
- Monetizing a *pro bono* speech from FREE to FEE
- Establishing your speaking fee
- Maximizing your value to get the gig
- Identifying an organization's level of budget
- Understanding the psychology of a speaking fee
- Creating speaking proposals, contracts and invoices

Module 5: Getting PAID Again
- Applying a consistent system
- Understanding your hunger
- Surrounding yourself with support
- Showing appreciation
- Giving and getting referrals
- Finding a speaking mentor
- Setting realistic expectations

Claim a complimentary coaching session

About the Author

BONUS Chapter: *How to Write a Book in 90 Days!*

Introduction

This book will teach you everything I know about how to be successful in the professional speaking business. Remember though, it's not what you *know*. It's what you *apply*.

The chapters of this book are written as coaching modules within my *PAID to Speak!*™ coaching program. Therefore, read with a pen in hand and be prepared to work as if each module were a coaching call. By holding yourself accountable to do so, you will gain tremendous momentum toward your speaking goals and aspirations.

Each of the modules has a unique focus and is designed to carefully guide you step-by-step through a systemized process that personalizes your objectives and helps you to identify a transparent strategy for speaking. If you speed through the chapters without completing the reflective questions and module checklist, you might as well drop a 100lb weight on your foot and start screaming. You will not benefit from this book unless you follow the system being recommended. I know it can work for you. It's worked for me and within six months, I had over a dozen keynotes lined up.

The only reason you do *not* complete the questions is because you plan to read the entire book first and are committed to reading the book *again* in order to complete the activities. From previous feedback with some coaching clients, this was a preferred approach. Also, many people have contacted me asking if I would coach and work with them through this book. I am happy to do so. Details on my PAID to SPEAK™ coaching program are on the final page of this book.

Important: This book is about PAID professional speaking. This book is *not* about *how* to SPEAK; rather it is about how to get PAID doing it. This is the reason you will notice I will capitalize PAID each and every time. Of course being a great public speaker will impact one's ability to be a professional speaker, and I will share some techniques and strategies that will make you stand out in the crowd. It is impossible to "fake it until you make it" on stage. Every time I hear that phrase, I cringe. I've never heard that phrase from someone who was successful either.

Note: Those who complete this book will receive a special gift. That gift is a complimentary 30-minute coaching call via phone – a value of $99. Your call is an opportunity to ask me, no holds barred, any questions for clarification that will help you personalize the content.

Module 1: Where to Start

<u>Question</u>: How do you eat an elephant?

<u>Answer</u>: One bite at a time!

This module will help you understand specifically where to start on this journey of professional speaking. In this chapter, you will:

- set your foundation of speaking through a series of reflective questions.
- understand the importance of an abundance mindset and realize there are speaking opportunities all over the world.

- learn the most critical components of a successful and engaging speech.
- you will discover how to differentiate and brand yourself as a speaker.

Module 2: Developing Your Program

In this module you will:
- identify, counter and break through the most common myths of the speaking business. These myths hold speakers back before they even get started.
- understand the most important document needed to confirm speaking engagements and review other items you need/do not need.
- learn how to design your presentation as a 'storyboard' to ensure you maximize your audience's engagement level and generate enthusiastic referrals.

"Success is when preparation meets opportunity." ~ Zig Ziglar

Module 3: Finding Opportunities & Getting Found

This module will ensure that you:
- identify speaking engagement opportunities like never before.
- understand what a marketing outreach strategy looks like.
- learn about how to speak to high school, college and university audiences.

- know how to maximize your ability to gain both referrals and inquiries.

Module 4: Getting PAID to SPEAK!

This module will share tips and ideas for how you will:
- monetize a *pro bono* speech.
- learn specific tips that will help you establish your speaking fee and front-load value that maximizes your bookings.
- understand the psychology of a speaking fee so that you never leave money on the table.
- craft speaking proposals, contracts and invoices.

Module 5: Getting PAID Again!

This module will:
- provide a collection of recommendations and concepts that will ensure you receive consistent PAID speaking bookings.
- teach you the importance of surrounding yourself with support.
- offer ideas for how to show appreciation to your clients.
- share strategies for both giving and receiving referrals.
- emphasize the importance of finding a speaking mentor.
- help you identify and set realistic expectations.

Upon completion of Chapter 5, contact me for a complimentary coaching call. Let's get started.

Author's Preface

My Story: How I became a speaker ...

At the beginning of my professional career, I worked in student affairs at several different colleges and universities. I felt great interest toward learning and teaching concepts of leadership and personal development to students. I absolutely loved facilitating small workshops on my campus – 20 students, at most, would attend. I had no intention or desire of becoming a speaker early on.

While attending leadership conferences with my students I would present these same small workshops as educational breakout sessions. I was never paid nor did I ever think about being compensated in any way.

One particular conference in 2001 changed my life. I remember listening to the welcome remarks from the conference organizer. I do not remember what they shared but I do recall them being extremely boring. If 'smart' phones existed back then, I would have been texting, checking email or searching the web randomly. I checked out quickly.

I checked back in when the opening keynote speaker was introduced. Music began to play, the energy skyrocketed and the speaker took the stage. Within the first 30 seconds, I was laughing and giving high five's to people sitting around me. One minute later, I was on my feet both giving and getting a back massage. I kept thinking, "This speaker is FUN!"

The opening keynote speaker commanded attention from the entire audience of 800 people for over an hour. What I remember most is relating to his stories, feeling inspired and laughing constantly. The speaker was not anyone particularly famous and he did not share any type of 'Mount Everest achievements' or 'near death' experiences. He was just extremely good connecting with his audience.

Half-way through the speaker's presentation, this voice in my head began saying, "I WANT to do this. I WANT to speak. I WANT to make an impact like this."

Right then and there I decided I was going to become a motivational speaker – whatever it took. My passion for speaking had become identified and unleashed all because of this one speaker.

When the keynote speaker finished, the audience responded with a standing ovation. The speaker more than deserved it.

My internal voice continued talking to me.

I approached the speaker and waited in line behind at least 50 people. When it was my turn to greet the speaker, I said, "Thank you, you made a difference for so many people today. I would love to talk with you about bringing you to my campus for a keynote presentation."

The speaker smiled and replied, "I'd be honored to speak at your campus."

Unexpectedly, the spirit moved me to keep talking and I added, "I also want to know how you became a speaker. I want to do what you do." It had not been my intention to ask about speaking. It somehow just came out of my mouth.

"Meet me for coffee in the lobby when I am finished here," the speaker said. "I'd be happy to talk with you about speaking and answer any questions."

My heart pounded with excitement. I could not believe this speaker was going to talk with me! I was both honored and humbled. I didn't even know what questions to ask or where to start.

I waited in the lobby for nearly an hour while the speaker continued shaking hands, and taking leads, from those who were in the audience. "Wow!" I kept thinking. "What a profession."

When the speaker finally sat down with me, we spoke for nearly an hour. He was as authentic and amazing 1-on-1 as he was on stage. What the speaker shared with me about how he got started as a speaker is the basis of what you are about to read in this book.

The most important common denominator both the speaker and I shared was a DESIRE to INSPIRE. That internal voice of mine saying, "I WANT to do that!" was fueled by a desire to make an impact.

Two hours later, I facilitated my own educational breakout session. The session was my normal workshop I had presented several dozen times in the past. However, I made a slight change to it this time.

Incorporating a piece of advice from the keynote speaker, I added a personal element to the workshop. I shared my *story* about how I lived a dream of being on, and winning, the game show *The Price is Right (TPIR)*. Being on TPIR had been a dream of mine since early childhood. After years of studying grocery prizes, analyzing how to play the games on the show, arranging my class schedule in college around the show and even skipping my college graduation to drive across the country to be on the show, I finally was able to achieve my dream – a vision – of meeting Bob Barker and being on *TPIR*.

I had never included this story in any previous presentation. I never really understood how my *healthy obsession* of meeting Bob Barker related to leadership. My story just seemed silly. What I soon became to understand though is that sharing your story differentiates you as a speaker. The more unique your story, the more people will remember you. Moreover, the more 'silly' your story is, the more engaged your audience likely will be.

Slightly apprehensive about adding my 5-minute segment of winning on *TPIR* in the workshop, I followed the speaker's recommendations and included it. I felt the fear but did it anyway. I connected the theme from my TPIR story to the overall workshop message of **(1) having a vision for what you want in life and (2) never giving up.**

The workshop was a huge success! Attendees seemed more engaged and excited than ever before. Presenting was more fun than it ever had been and the interaction was phenomenal. As attendees left the room, several stopped to thank me. Normally a few students would talk with me afterwards but this time was different. There was a line of them waiting!

I observed a young lady standing in the back of the room. She appeared shy and uncomfortable. I quickly realized she was waiting for everyone else to leave. We made eye contact a few times and I knew there was something important she wanted to say to me.

She finally approached me once the room had cleared. She seemed slightly nervous.

"Mr. Snyder," she said with a tentative smile. "That...that, was an incredible presentation." She paused and looked down.

"Well thank you. That's very kind," I replied. "What's your name?"

"My name is Karen," she said. She paused again. I could sense she was struggling for words. A few moments later she continued, "I want you to know that your presentation today really made an impact on me. It got me thinking."

"Oh really?" I said. "What did you enjoy most about it? How did it get you thinking?"

Something triggered in Karen and she shut down. She took a step back and looked away. Her face turned slightly pale and I could tell she was uncomfortable talking further. There was more she wanted to share yet she seemed conflicted on how, or if, to say what was really on her mind.

"Just about stuff," she said. "I have a lot of stuff I'm dealing with right now." I noticed that both times she said the word 'stuff' she looked away. Before I could ask her anything else, she turned to walk away, heading out the door.

As she walked out, I called out, "Thank you Karen." I felt I would hear from her again at some point. I was convinced there was more. I finished packing up my workshop materials and left the room.

Later that day I was standing in the conference hotel lobby. An older gentleman approached me with a smile and asked, "Are you *The Price Is Right* guy?"

"*The Price Is Right* guy?" I thought to myself. I was confused. I had never heard that phrase before.

"*The Price Is Right*?" I replied to the man. "Uhhmmm. I was on the show. How did you know?

He continued in an enthusiastic tone, "You made a presentation earlier today didn't you? And you spoke about your dream growing up to meet Bob Barker and be on *The Price Is Right*?"

"That was me," I said, smiling.

"Wow!" he replied. "My students have been raving about you all day and I wanted you to know. We have a student leadership conference in a few months and we want you to be our keynote speaker. We'd love for you to share the same story. Oh, and by the way, my name is Mike."

Mike didn't know it, but he has just given me my first keynote presentation opportunity.

Trying not to seem the amateur I was then by showing too much excitement, I smiled and replied, "I'd love that opportunity. Thank you Mike. And by the way, my name is Kevin Snyder."

"Wonderful, Kevin. I'll contact you soon for more details. But just remember, we want to hear *The Price Is Right* story that you shared today. Our students will love you."

As we exchanged business cards, we made small talk for a few moments. He then inquired, "Oh, one more thing." He paused. "What's your speaking fee?"

I felt like I had been jolted with a mini bolt of lightning. "Uh oh," I thought to myself. "My fee? I don't even have a fee. I didn't expect this. What do speakers even charge?"

"Uhm…uhm…uhm," I stuttered. "Mind if I get back to you on that? I just need a few more details from you first."

Mike seemed a bit surprised I was not prepared to quote a fee. I am confident at that point he sensed that I was a newbie in the field of speaking. I certainly felt that way. In fact, I am sure that a vibe of 'speaker amateur' was oozing from every pore in my body.

"Sure thing Kevin," he said. "We'll talk very soon." Mike then turned and walked away.

I turned around and mentally jumped up and down clicking my heels together. "My first gig! I cannot believe it!" I was thrilled. That was one of the happiest days of my life.

But now I had a problem. Not only did I have to organize my workshop presentation into a keynote speech, which I had no clue how to do, I also had to determine a fee and write a contract. Would I be engaging enough? What was my worth? I did not know where to start. (Side note: We'll be covering these issues in this book.)

Throughout that evening at the conference event, random people kept approaching me with a smile and inquiring if I was *'The Price Is Right* guy'. Although I must admit the attention was inspiring, it felt plain odd. I didn't expect any of this. Frankly, I wasn't sure I liked that nickname -*'The Price Is Right* guy.' It did seem to stick well though and it was unique.

The following morning I checked my email. I had a message from Karen, the student from the previous day who was hesitant talking to me. Her message began with:

> *Dear Mr. Snyder, you probably don't remember me but .....*

Of course I remembered her! In fact, I had expected to hear from her in some way. As I read her message, my jaw dropped and my eyes became misty. She wrote that my presentation had helped her with a desire to change her life. My story of being on *The Price Is Right* also equipped her with a vision for healing and moving onward in a positive direction. In her email, Karen informed me that for as long as she could remember, she suffered from depression and bipolar disorder, had been in and out of rehabilitation clinics and foster care homes, was bulimic, a cutter, and had attempted suicide on multiple occasions.

A tear rolled down my cheek when I read that she had attended the conference in order to end it all. She was planning on killing herself - this time being far away from anyone who could help her – and being successful.

Karen wrote, "Something about your presentation got me thinking different about my own life and that I could make a change …you saved my life."

"I saved her life?" I thought. "No way. Not my silly little story." I could neither understand or describe the emotions I felt. I was humbled that I - or rather my presentation content - could have such an impact on someone.

I also thought to myself, "She has no clue how similar she and I are. How ironic." You see, despite me - *Mr. Motivation Boy* – seeming confident and collected while facilitating in front of a group of people, Karen did not know that I had dealt with very similar issues growing up.

I had suffered from depression through my teenage years, was a clinically diagnosed anorexic, had run away from home a few times, had strongly considered suicide on multiple occasions, and had even been arrested. Karen had no clue about any of that. How could she?

What I immediately realized sitting alone in my hotel room was that whether by accident or by divine intention, people relate much more to your struggle than your strength. When they know you have been there, you are more relatable. Period. As a speaker, when you share your story of struggle and perseverance, your audience knows you have been tested and are more open to hearing what you did to get better and become successful. After all, they assume you are speaking to them for a reason. This is yet another reason for sharing your story. It not only will differentiate you, but will also carry your powerful message.

I thanked Karen for her message and asked if she felt comfortable talking with me in the hotel lobby over coffee. During our conversation, I applauded her for demonstrating strength by talking with me. I also told her briefly about my struggles and how she and I had much more common than she realized. Her eyes became misty while listening to me tell about my depression, suicidal thoughts and arrest. She also agreed to talk with a counselor when she got back to campus.

Karen and I have kept in touch since that day. In fact, she is aware of my dedication to her in this book. The dedication is always the first portion of every book I write. It anchors me to *why* the book is being written. When you know your *why*, it makes everything else more evident.

Karen earned her Masters degree in psychology and is now a college counselor. I will not be surprised to hear of her becoming a Dean of Students or Vice President of Student Affairs one day in the future. Perhaps she just might even be a keynote speaker.

After my conversation with Karen in the lobby, there was a closing session to conclude the conference and send us all on our way back home. I walked inside the ballroom and took my seat at a table with my students. One of my students immediately shouted out loud, "*The Price Is Right* guy!"

We all laughed. My own students had somehow heard of my new nickname and were happy to let me know they would carry it back home to our campus as well.

Lunch began and several awards were given out. One of the awards was 'Best Presentation' which recognized the highest evaluated session from over 150 educational breakout sessions at the conference. I didn't think I had a shot. In fact, being in the top 20 wasn't on my mind ... that is, until I heard my name being called out to receive the award.

"Mr. Kevin Snyder," the emcee announced into the microphone in front of over 800 people. "Please come to the stage to receive your 'Best Presentation' award.

I felt nothing but numbness as I walked toward the front and onto that stage. As the emcee and I shook hands and smiled for the camera, I remember feeling a sense of connection to that stage. It is still so difficult to describe other than just emphasizing how natural and right it felt. My legs felt like tree roots and new seeds had been planted on that stage. I felt destined to be a speaker.

Sitting back down at my table, I received hugs from all of my students. I think they were as surprised as I was about the award. I passed the award around and when it came full circle back to me, I held it in my lap mesmerized by **Best Presentation Award** in laser etching.

After all the awards had been given out, the emcee announced, "Before we conclude, it is my privilege to introduce our closing keynote speaker."

"Awesome!" I thought. "Another keynote speaker!" Whereas most people would be gritting their teeth wanting to leave, I was ecstatic about hearing from another keynote speaker. If he was anything like the opening speaker, we were in for an incredible treat. I was already rooting for him even before he began speaking.

Unfortunately, he was *nothing* like the opening speaker. In fact, he was absolutely horrible, being everything the other speaker wasn't. The closing speaker did nothing interactive during the presentation, spoke about himself quite a bit, had no audience laughter, used bullet-pointed Power Point slides and used a few jokes that did not work. I could go on and on. Point is, he never engaged the audience and he didn't have a clear message.

Within the first 15 minutes, that internal voice inside me said, "I CAN do this. I CAN be a speaker."

The opening keynote speaker at that conference helped instill a desire for speaking inside me – the 'I WANT to be a speaker' factor. And just as important, the closing speaker instilled a different belief inside me – the 'I CAN be a speaker' factor. Both are important. You must have the desire but you also must have the hunger and belief in yourself.

So it began. When I returned home, I proudly displayed my 'Best Presentation' award in my living room and began working on the recommendations given to me by the first opening speaker. I bought several books on how to become a speaker and unleashed myself into this new arena of life. My aspirations of becoming a speaker began with the end in mind.

It was not easy though. In fact, looking back, what I wish I would have done is find a coach and more speaking mentors to guide me consistently along the way. I struggled putting concepts together in keynote form, finding consistent opportunities to speak, and knowing where to market my presentation. I still worked a full time job in student affairs while developing my speaking business.

For the first few years, I averaged roughly 10-15 speaking gigs a year. I seemed to hover around this number and could not grow it further. I remember becoming frustrated at times because I knew I was destined to speak more. I felt a connection to my audiences, to the stage and to the message I was sharing. I did not realize it at the time, but I was developing a *system for speaking*. The book you hold in your hands is that system in tangible, written form. It's what I did, and continue to do, in order to secure paid speaking opportunities. My speaking business exploded once this system became clear and I took action.

Since my first keynote speaking at Mike's campus 14 years ago, I have keynoted over 1,000 presentations spanning all 50 states and several countries. I have spoken at over 500 colleges and universities as well as hundreds of high schools, associations, corporate organizations, churches, and many more groups. Roughly half my current speaking is with college audiences and the other half focuses on my corporate/professional organizations. More about my speaking and niche audiences can be found at the conclusion of this book.

I felt it was important to share with you how I started as a speaker. It wasn't pretty and although I had a general direction of what I wanted to achieve, I figured most of the speaking business out the hard and long way. However, my journey was fueled by a passionate desire and knowledge from others who served as mentors for me. Along the way, I progressed and am humbly proud to have made an impact in people's lives.

Why I wrote this book is a different story ...

The genesis of this book sources from the numerous times I have been asked by other aspiring speakers, "So how did you become a speaker?"

I was happy to answer this question over coffee when I first moved to Raleigh, North Carolina several years ago. I was a successful speaker but also new in town. I knew no one. I was interested in meeting new people, networking, and further expanding my speaking business. However, after coffee chats with at least 50 people, I recognized several patterns that finally forced me to reflect and realize I knew more about the speaking business than I thought. The strategies about the business of speaking that seemed obvious to me now were not so obvious to others. I became aware of three patterns:

Pattern #1: I started getting asked the same questions over and over ... and over. Here's a short list:

How do you get paid to speak?
Who books speakers?
Is there a specific topic that is best to speak about?
How do you get hired to speak on college campuses?

Should I speak for free?
How do you set your fee?
Should I hire an agent or speakers bureau?

Tip: When you start being asked the same question, or questions, repeatedly, the universe is telling you something. It means you know something that others do not. More importantly, it means your knowledge can help.

I was happy to answer these questions and support their aspirations of becoming a speaker. However, when pattern #2 emerged, I started becoming frustrated.

Pattern #2: Those aspiring speakers I met with did nothing with my advice.

Our conversations about *their interest* in becoming a speaker did not lead anywhere. In the spirit of further building our relationship, I would meet with people again perhaps 1-2 months later or I would bump into them at an event. I would ask, "So how's speaking going?"

Though I was assuming they had applied a few of the recommendations we discussed, I consistently heard, "Oh well … you know, things have been really busy … <insert excuses here> …" Meaning, nothing had been done, or at best very little.

Here I was sharing important and helpful advice, as well as valuable time, in hopes it would help them move forward toward their speaking aspirations. After all, our conversations had focused on their hopes. However, when no progress was the consistent common denominator, I realized both their time and mine had been wasted.

Note: This might sound like I had unrealistic expectations, but most of those people I met with were business owners, consultants and entrepreneurs. I expected a bit more action from those who talked about strategy and action in their business.

Identifying that the coffee conversations yielded only minimal action, I stepped back from agreeing to coffee chats about speaking and went in a different direction. I coordinated a workshop on speaking, attached a small price tag of $49 for room/supplies and cast out a net of invitations. I did not even have a name for the workshop so I called it "How To Become A Speaker Workshop." Looking back this was amateurish effort but it reaped amazing results.

To my surprise 33 aspiring speakers attended this 'amateur' workshop. Moreover, what was scheduled to only be a 2-hour workshop ended up being 3.5 hours and people followed me to my car asking about one-on-one coaching services. I resisted the coaching and turned opportunities down. Well, what you resist, persists.

Pattern #3: Feedback from the speaker workshop evaluations, although extremely positive, helped me recognize that attendees were still hungry for more. Most still seemed to lack clarity and a clear strategy for where to start. It was then that I thought about developing a more clear system to help people become speakers. That written system is what you have in your hand.

Because every speech, every speaker and every industry is unique, each person needs a customized approach. One size does NOT fit all. Every audience is different. Furthermore, speakers have different stories, help audiences in different ways, and frankly, speak in different ways.

What you are reading now took me 14 years to understand. I am confident that what took me 14 years to accomplish should take you four months if you follow the system I share. It's up to you. It's not what you know, it's what you apply. This system works and I am reminded of that each time I receive a speaking gig.

To your success as well!

To Your Continued Success,

~ *Kevin*

"The most important criteria for determining whether or not you achieve your speaking goals is that you already have a vision and hunger for achieving them. Everything else is just a matter of time."

MODULE 1: WHERE TO START?

"It all begins first with a dream." ~ Walt Disney

I recognize that each of you reading this book comes with a different set of experiences, interests and backgrounds. You desire to speak for different reasons and you have distinctive personal stories motivating you to open this book to begin with. I applaud your interest and I am looking forward to hearing of your development and future success.

The greatest inventions of all time have a common denominator. That is, they each started with the same thing – a vision. That vision evolved and distilled itself into actionable goals with strategic legs and timelines. A career in speaking is no different. The journey must start with a vision. You have to have a vision - a dream - for what you to want to accomplish. As Walt Disney said, "It all begins first with a dream."

For me personally, my vision for speaking was born by watching a phenomenal speaker (see Author's Preface) when I said to myself, "I WANT to do that!" That speaker helped me establish a vision for doing exactly what he was doing. That vision anchored my planning for years as I worked extremely hard to build my speaking business. Even when I finally manifested that reality I did not stop. I continued to envision the next higher level I wanted to achieve. Even now I continue to create new visions for my speaking career. These visions are what guide and motivate me to stretch my speaking goals and perpetually advance. They are expectations for what is to come. If I don't vision something, I don't make it a goal.

Having a vision for speaking is imperative for your speaking success. You have to begin with the end in mind. The more clear your vision for speaking the more likely you will achieve that outcome. Below is a series of broad questions to help you attain clarity on what your vision to become a speaker looks like. As you reflect and answer these questions, picture yourself being five years old and feeling as if anything is possible. Do not put limits on yourself. Go BIG or go HOME. The more clear and descriptive your visions are the more likely you will attain them.

<u>Describe your overall vision for speaking. What do you want to accomplish through speaking</u>?

Envision you just completed a speech in front of an audience. One of the attendees approaches you afterward and gives you amazing feedback about your presentation. Write down what they are saying:

Are you being hired to speak? Or is your speaking designed to market a product or service that you offer?

How do you want to inspire others through speaking?

Do you want to speak in front of large audiences (500-1,000+) or do you prefer speaking in smaller group audiences (< 100)? Or both?

Describe your average audience participant. Who are they?

What frequency of speaking would you like? Twice a week, once a week, once a month, etc.?

<u>Are you bound by geography or would you be open to traveling across the country/globe</u>?

Unless you plan to re-read this book, it is recommended that you do not continue until you have answered the previous questions.
Please go back and complete any unanswered questions.

The questions above are designed to help get your creative juices flowing. Exploring the possibilities as well as identifying any limitations for your speaking career is fundamental to your success.

At the time of this publication, I am neither married nor do I have children. My personal circumstances allow me to speak wherever and whenever opportunities arise. My only real limitation is availability. Let me provide you with a real-life example of why defining the boundaries of your vision is so paramount:

A 3-day Tour: A few years ago I hosted one of my *PAID to SPEAK!*™ seminars and invited interested attendees to join me on an upcoming speaking 'tour' that following month. I had been booked for three consecutive days of speaking with different groups and I thought it would be interesting for the seminar attendees to experience all the behind-the-scene details of a speaking tour. The plan was to fly in on Sunday evening, speak to one group on Monday, speak to another on Tuesday, another on Wednesday and fly out Wednesday evening. Three seminar attendees came with me which made me thrilled – in addition to their camaraderie, I planned to use their help with video recording, event set up and book sales.

The first day of speaking was exciting. We had flown in the night before and had a one-hour drive from the airport. We each woke that morning at 6am to be onsite at the client conference and ready by 10am. The keynote was scheduled for noon and it went phenomenally well with a very receptive audience. Following the keynote we had two hours of book sales and mingling. Finally at about 3:00pm we packed up and began the two-hour drive to the next day's presentation city. We checked into the hotel about 5:30pm and then visited the conference center ballroom where the following day's morning keynote was going to take place. (*Tip: Always view your location/venue setting as far in advance as possible. It will help you with visioning your speech delivery*.) At about 6:30pm we relaxed and strategized over dinner. I then returned to my room to review my notes for the next day's keynote and evening breakout sessions and went to bed about 11:00pm.

We woke up that Tuesday morning at 6:00 to be downstairs and ready by 8:00 for the 10:00am opening keynote presentation. The keynote went extremely well and the audience seemed quite engaged. We spent the following two hours on book sales and mingling. Then there was a conference lunch followed by two breakout workshops I had agreed to facilitate. The conference concluded by 4:30pm and we were packed up and leaving by 6:00.

We hit the road and drove three hours to the next city, arriving that evening about 9:00. After checking into the hotel and visiting the ballroom where the conference was to be held, we ate a late dinner and were back in our separate hotel rooms by 11:00pm. I stayed up until 1:00am reviewing the morning's keynote and additional breakout presentation. Just like the day before, we woke up that Wednesday morning at 6:00 to be downstairs and ready by 8:30 for the 11:00am keynote presentation.

Wednesday's keynote also went extremely well and I facilitated my breakout session from 2:00-3:00pm. Following the breakout session, we mingled for a bit and then packed up near 4:00pm. We drove two hours to catch our evening flight from Texas back to North Carolina. While waiting for our flight, I was surprised to hear two of them talk about how *they* were exhausted. Sparing you our dialogue, I will share this remark from one of them: "We did not expect this to be so much work. These were 15-hour days!" I kept silent, apprehensive of what might come from my mouth. I finally responded to them, smiling, "It's not work when you love what you do."

I checked back in with each of them the following week to hear how they were feeling about our previous week's 'tour.' I wasn't surprised to hear that the two individuals who related speaking to work told me they felt speaking was not for them. Experiencing all the pre-logistics and onsite details seemed to have overwhelmed and intimidated them. They both also shared with me that, as mothers, they did not want to travel that intense nor did they want to be far away from their families for more than one day a week. One of them also shared with me that her daughter became ill while being away and she felt absolutely horrible about not being there for her.

I share this story with you for a variety of reasons. Know that speaking requires incredible investment and work. Building your paid speaking business will likely be one of the toughest things you have ever done. Beginning with the end in mind though, it should not be work. Consider it a new adventure. Additionally, know that some weeks will just seem crazy. You are preparing for one gig right after the other. Some days you might be speaking two or three times. That might seem exciting and appealing now, but when you're in the moment, tired from traveling and having to be 'on,' it can seem daunting.

Be clear about what your vision for speaking looks like. Do you have geographic or schedule limitations? Do you want to travel? Are you prepared to be away from your family at times? Do you desire to speak just once per week or would you prefer to only travel once or twice per month? These are all extremely important factors.

What Is Professional Speaking?

Although the focus of this book will be on keynote speaking, you can be PAID to SPEAK in a variety of formats. For example, I have been hired as a keynote speaker for hundreds of conferences and special events. I also have been paid to be an emcee, an auctioneer, small group workshop presenter, full day retreat leader, board meeting facilitator and even have conducted my *PAID to SPEAK*™ seminars for organizational leaders and their internal employees. When people see you speak and they are captivated by your energy and content, they will be thinking of creative ways to use you. You want them thinking, "Wow, this speaker would be great for our _____." Point is that you could be hired to speak in a variety of formats, venues and environments. Be prepared for random requests!

Keynote speaking is unique because people are listening to you, and only you, for a specified period of time. Most likely you will be on a stage, or at least in front of a room, and you will be speaking for roughly an hour. You might be asked to speak for less or more time depending on venue, environment and objective. Audience sizes range as well – from a handful of 15-20 people to thousands. When I speak at conferences, my most common audience size ranges from 400-600 people. My largest audience has topped 5,000 and my smallest was three attendees. I was PAID the same amount for both keynote speeches and it was the same speech! As I will explain in later modules, I have a daily fee regardless of attendee size, length of speech and location.

Envision yourself speaking in front of a large group. Is that the type of setting you desire? If not, what is the setting you desire? This goes back to the first question I presented to you in this module – what is your vision?

Three Most Important Questions

Regardless of the type of speech you are asked to give, there are four core fundamentals that any keynote, workshop or retreat must incorporate. Those are that your speech must be:

- **extremely engaging,**
- **share a powerful message,**
- **integrate personal/relative stories and examples and**
- **leave attendees with an empowering Call to Action.**

This segment will provide three questions whose answers will ensure your speaking foundation is built correctly on those fundamentals. Through experiences of my own and many others, I have found that being able to answer these questions will keep you focused on not only developing a tailored program that gets referrals but also identifying the best industries and organizations for you to seek speaking engagements. If I had focused on these three questions years ago, I would have been much more successful in significantly less time. When I realized the importance of the answers to the three questions below, my speaking business exploded.

Question 1: What problem do you want to help others solve?

Explanation: As a speaker, you are not being hired to SPEAK. Rather, you are hired to share a message that will help a company, association and/or attendees solve a specific, or series, of problems. *It ain't about you*. Rather, it's about your message and how the content empowers the attendees. Develop your presentation around your message of how you plan to help them solve a problem.

<u>In the space provided below, describe what problem you want to help attendees solve</u>:

Question 2: What makes you different as compared to another SPEAKER on a similar topic?

Explanation: There are lots of speakers, but only one you. How you are different is what will make you remembered. Your uniqueness is what differentiates you. Be different. Be so good they cannot forget you. As I previously mentioned, share a unique story that only you have. For example, I've been called *"The Price Is Right (TPIR) guy"* to my face countless times - behind my back likely thousands - but that's a good thing because people remember me for that story. As you read in the preface, that story literally launched my speaking career. I've been stopped on campuses, at conferences and even in airports by people asking, "You're that speaker who was on *The Price Is Right*?" I love it.

My story of being on TPIR isn't about how to win on a game show; rather, it's about how to live a dream and that is the message communicated through my presentations. Anything is possible when you set your mind to it with a healthy obsession. Thousands of other people have been on *TPIR*, but no one on this planet has my signature story. It's what makes me – just like you and your story - different. Our story anchors our message. Our story helps liven our speeches and keeps the presentation engaging.

In the space provided below, write what you feel makes you different from other speakers on a similar topic? What differentiates you?

What is your story?

Question 3: What is your Call to Action?

Explanation: This is by far where most speakers, even professionals, fall painfully short. What do you want your audiences to do differently as a result of hearing your message? Your Call to Action is what clearly inspires attendees to take action toward something. Most speakers I have seen do not have a clear Call to Action, or any at all.

In order for your attendees to know what your Call to Action is you must tell them specifically. Do not let them wonder. Be transparently clear. If your presentation does not inspire them to make a change in their personal life and/or business, then you have wasted your time. More importantly, you've wasted theirs and, as a not-so-surprising result, the likelihood of you getting referrals and spin-off speaking inquiries will be minimal.

<u>In the space provided below, list all the action steps you would like your attendees to do differently as a result of hearing you speak. Then, review these in detail and look for one theme or pattern – this is your specific Call to Action!</u>

Write your Call to Action below!

So What Do You SPEAK On?

Envision this scenario. I am a professional meeting planner for a major association and you are a speaker. You and I have just met, sitting next to each other on a plane. We make small talk for a few moments and then exchange names. The likely question I am going to ask you at some point is, "So, what do you do?"

This is one of the ultimate questions you need to be prepared for.

You reply that you are a professional speaker. After hearing your response, I'll likely inquire further. Consider the dialogue below:

"Oh really," I'll respond. "So what do you speak on?"

You look away to the left and then back at me, responding "Well, uhmm … I speak about <u>business leadership</u>." (or insert your topic here)

I'll likely probe a bit further because I have a need for a speaker at our upcoming convention, so I'll ask, "What about business leadership?"

"Well, uhmm …" you reply again.

Our exchange occurs this quickly, and also my interest in you. When I hear the words "Well uhmm," it makes a statement far greater than the statement itself. Do not let this happen to you. Be prepared. You very likely just lost an opportunity for a speaking engagement because you do not seem to be clear on your own speaking topic. If I were a professional meeting planner or conference organizer, your lack of an answer tells me that you are likely not the professional speaker I need for my big event coming up.

However, if you were prepared to answer that question, you'd immediately capture my interest and likely close the deal. Point is, know what it is you speak on anticipate that question! Also, be able to answer that question in one sentence or less.

I cannot count the number of times I have been asked, "What do you speak on?" This question always arises whether I am on an airplane, at a conference where attendees have not seen me speak yet, waiting in line at random locations, at a networking event, at church, etc. This is by far the most common question I receive from people when I tell them I speak for a living.

Let's assume now that the roles are reversed and I am sitting next to you on that plane. You ask me, "So what do you speak on?"

I would answer that question in a way that would compel you to further inquire with yet another question. The more you talk and inquire the better.

My reply, "In my presentations I share success secrets of high performing leaders and organizations and specifically, what they do differently."

What would your response be to my answer?

Likely your response would be another question:

"Really? Give me an example."
"What are some of the topics you speak on?"
"Who are some groups you speak to?"

Important: Depending on who I think you are will determine my answer. It also depends where we are. For example, if we are at a professional conference for a certain industry, at a networking event with business entrepreneurs, or at a collegiate leadership conference, I will at least vaguely know what type of career you are in. Therefore, my responses might be, "I speak on topics of leadership and innovation that help organizations empower and engage their employees." Or I might say, "I speak to college students about how to identify their passions in life and be exceptional leaders."

What I want you to remember is this:

"Always leave them with a desire to ask you another question."

In the space provided below, write down three ways you could answer the following question, "So what do you speak on?"

Module Review

In this module, you have:
- **gained clarity in your vision for speaking,**
- **forecasted possible speaking limitations,**
- **reflected on what differentiates you as a speaker,**
- **understood the power of your message, story and call to action and**
- **have developed a powerful answer for when you are asked, "So what do you speak on?"**

If you have completed all the reflective questions in this module to your own satisfaction, then congratulations! You are ready for Module 2! However, if any portions are missing, I highly recommend you go back and complete them now. You will not be following this *PAID to SPEAK™* system by speeding through this book. When you contact me to set up your complimentary coaching call, the first question I ask will be, "Did you complete each question in the book?" Remember, what you are reading is designed to be a coaching manual as well as a narrated version of my seminar. Be your own accountability coach and complete the activities if you have not done so already! The checklist on the next page will help ensure you are ready.

"If you don't have time to do it now, when will you have time to do it again?

MODULE 1 CHECKLIST

	YES	NO
I feel confident about my vision for speaking.	____	____
I have reflected on possible limitations and I have clarity on frequency/geography.	____	____
I am clearer about the different types of formats I could be PAID to SPEAK.	____	____
I know what problem I am helping solve.	____	____
I know what differentiates me as a speaker.	____	____
I have a signature story to share.	____	____
I understand what my Call to Action will be.	____	____
When someone asks me what I speak on, I now have a powerful answer.	____	____

If you have checked 'YES' on all the items above, proceed to Module 2!

NOTES

NOTES

NOTES

Module 2: Developing Your Program

I hear all the excuses in the world about why speakers struggle when they get started. They make assumptions about what the business is like and reasons why they aren't getting booked:

"I have to have a bureau represent me."
"I need to have a book."
"They aren't returning my phone call."
"They don't have any money."
"I need a better website/marketing video/flier."

While some of these statements may have relevance later down the road on higher level speaking engagements, do not focus on them right now. They are **common speaker myths** that should not be allowed to get in your way as you get started.

To get started, you need belief in what problem you solve and an incredible presentation to share that message. You will never get booked as a speaker unless you first have a great program, i.e. presentation. Your presentation gets booked, not you. That is, unless you are a famous speaker the like of Anthony Robbins, Les Brown, John Maxwell, Wayne Dyer or Tom Hopkins and your name precedes you. If you are someone famous, I am shocked - yet pleasantly surprised - you are reading this book!

I would encourage you to have two or three programs eventually, but let's start with getting your first program solidified and nailed solid. Chase one squirrel at a time. Chase more than one squirrel at a time and you will catch none. Focus on one. I have found that most people chase squirrels and shiny objects all over the place. Then they blame circumstances and wonder why they were not successful. It comes down to focus.

Later in this chapter we will go in more depth on how to design your presentation, both in 'puzzle piece' outline nuggets and in aesthetics, and I will provide you with tips that will help you differentiate yourself from other speakers in your field.

Let's be clear here - your program is what you speak on and it articulates your purpose for speaking. Your purpose should be the problem you are helping audience participants solve (Chapter 1). Your program includes several important components such as a title, a program description and at least two learning outcomes. All of this information, including a biography, headshot and contact information, should fit onto one page – called your *One Page*. Consider it your marketing page that gives a conference organizer/meeting planner everything they need to review your speech.

Whether someone is inquiring with me about a speaking opportunity or I am submitting a "Call for Programs" to speak at a conference, these elements in my *One Page* are always required. (Note: "Call for Programs" are defined as what conference organizers announce when they are seeking speaker submissions. Commonly, these are for educational sessions, not keynotes. These phrases might also be called "Call for Speakers" or "Call for Presenters.")

I have never been asked to speak where at least a presentation title, description and bio were not needed. Having these elements available immediately and upfront sets you apart, makes you appear professional and saves you considerable amounts of time. I can submit a conference call for programs within 15 minutes because I have my presentation content already available.

Your program **should always be tailored** for the industry and audience you are speaking. If you are speaking at a conference and they have a theme, tweak your program to fit. In fact, I have had dozens of occasions where a conference theme was set around my keynote title and/or book! The attendees likely did not know this, but the meeting planner/conference organizer loved me for it.

Important: When you tweak your presentation title and/or description, you do not have to change considerably much content – hence the word tweak. If more than a tweak was needed, I would call it a new keynote. Just adjust it ever so slightly so that the person(s) reviewing your proposal feels as though your presentation was created just for them. Your goal is to make them feel that way and say to themselves, "Wow, this presentation is exactly what I'm looking for!"

Example #1: I recently was encouraged to apply for a speaker slot at a prestigious conference. I decided to tailor one of my common leadership presentations around both the conference theme and the industry itself. I simply took ten minutes to review their website and I wrote down and reflected on what I felt would most appeal to the people reviewing my presentation. With this information in mind, I made a few simple tweaks to tailor my presentation description and submitted it online. I knew my proposal would be compared to 20 other proposals for that one speaking spot. I heard back two weeks later that my program was accepted.

Example #2*:* I received an email from a former coaching client who speaks specifically to that type of industry. Surprisingly they were denied. This person was frustrated and inquired about my submission status. I mentioned that my presentation had been accepted. I asked if they tailored their presentation for the conference or if it was one of their common programs also listed on their website. What do you think their answer was? You likely guessed right – their submission had not been tailored whatsoever. They took the easy approach and submitted the same presentation off their website without tailoring it for the unique conference theme. The presentation reviewers likely recognized this lack of attention and effort as well.

Takeaway: Always tailor. It shows you care and ensures you stand out.

Whether you are submitting a call for programs or you already have the gig and they are contacting you with an inquiry, tailoring your program goes a long way. It shows you care and you are willing to stay fresh and current in your topic. It's the little things sometimes that make a big difference. And remember, it doesn't take long! You might even surprise yourself and develop a new keynote through the tweak.

Presentation Title

So let's start with a softball – **your presentation title.** Do you have one? Remember, depending on where you are at in your speaking career, you might have several programs. For right now though, let's focus on one presentation. Follow my advice on this so I can take you to the next level. Chase only one squirrel at a time.

If you do not have a presentation title, think about what your title might be. It will not be set in stone at this point and it will likely be modified depending on the type of group you are speaking to and if they have a conference theme. Furthermore, if you have several programs, choose only one right now. If you are not sure what presentation title to move forward with, consider these tips below:

Tips:

- I recommend looking at comparable speakers for your topic and their presentation titles. Do NOT copycat. Do this *only* to generate ideas.
- Find a conference schedule, likely online, of an industry where you would like to speak. Review their published programs and study the dozens of presentation titles that were accepted. (This is also helpful when drafting the description.)
- Write out title ideas and show them to a few of your close friends or business acquaintances. Get feedback. <u>Note</u>: Always be open to feedback when you ask for it.
- Share titles with me. When you complete this book and earn your coaching call, I will provide feedback as well. Asking for your program information will be one of the first things I ask you for in advance!

<u>Below are a few of my most common presentation titles</u>:
"How to Think Differently ... and Achieve Success"
"Engaging The New Frontier: How Millennials Are Changing The Workforce!"
"How to Empower Your Employees: Successful Engagement Leaves Clues!"
"The Ripple Effect: How To Inspire and Lead Transformational Change!'
"Unstoppable: Extraordinary Leadership Principles Driving Performance!"

As you can see, I have developed a variety of programs. In fact, I often send my 'menu' of programs – listed in my **One Page** – to those who inquire with me for speaking. I allow them to choose which presentation title sounds most interesting. They know their industry, group and attendees better than I do. Once I am informed which title is most appealing to them, then I consider how to tailor the title and description to meet their needs and objectives. As you build your speaking business you'll be able to do this as well.

Write below the title of your presentation - or at least write ideas for a title:

I do not recommend continuing onward until you at least have one presentation title to work with.

Presentation Description

Congratulations, we have your presentation title to work with! Now we continue with your presentation description. Your description should capture the essence of your presentation and include your purpose, what problem you will solve and the Call to Action (Chapter 1). You want your description to be both catchy and powerful.

Envision your presentation being compared to 20 other presentations for the same speaking slot. It likely will be - make it good! You also want to envision being a conference attendee and comparing your presentation description to the others in the same educational session block. What would make your description so appealing that attendees feel they must attend yours? Keeping these two reference points in mind will aid you in describing your presentation articulately and powerfully.

I recommend two different types of descriptions; one description under 80 words and another under 150 words. Why do you think I make that recommendation?

Most "Call for Programs" require a description of 80 words or fewer because word count is based on space available in the conference program. Moreover, readers should be able to understand your point within 80 words. If you cannot fit your description within 80 words, find someone who will help you cut content and make it concise. Sometimes though, a call for programs announcement/organizer/planner might ask for a longer description – it all depends. Remember, the speaking business is not *one size fits all*. Be prepared for anything. By having both short and long descriptions available you can respond more quickly and professionally.

Still focusing on one presentation and the title you just created, let's move forward with creating your description. Start with just writing phrases, one-liners and sentences you feel best describe your presentation. Once you accomplish this, begin writing out a concise description keeping it about 120 words for now. We can adjust the length later so that you have one presentation description under 80 words and another under 150 words. What we need now is a good description to work with.

In your description, be sure to state a problem/issue, how your presentation will address this issue and what attendees will learn from your presentation. Your description should reference both the industry and your learning outcomes in some fashion.

Do not rush this process. Most of the speakers I work with take at least a week or two to complete this assignment – some need longer because they are reflecting on questions I posed to them from Module 1 – i.e. problem to solve, call to action, story differentiation. You should follow the same tips as you did earlier for creating presentation titles and review your description over and over, tweaking and modifying it until you are satisfied.

Below is a sample presentation description of my Millennial program, "Engaging The New Frontier: How Millennials Are Changing The Workforce." I'll share with you my shortened description (< 80 words), the longer description (< 150 words) and the tailored version from the marketing conference I referenced earlier.

< 80 words:

A new generation of professionals has emerged, officially becoming the majority workforce demographic. This population known as Generation Y, or Millennials, is changing how organizations attract, develop, retain, and engage cross-generational employees. Organizations that understand the needs of Generation Y will find success in a more engaged workforce and also avoid significant costs of rapid employee turnover. In this interactive presentation, you will learn how this civic-minded and tech-savvy generation has impacted workplace culture and the way work gets done.

< 150 words:

A new generation of professionals has emerged and officially become the majority workforce demographic. This population known as Generation Y, or Millennials, is changing how human resource professionals, executives and managers foster an organizational culture that attracts, develops, retains, and engages cross-generational employees both now and in the future. Organizations that understand and embrace the needs and perspectives of Generation Y will not only find success in a more engaged and productive workforce, but also avoid significant costs of rapid employee turnover and disengagement. In this interactive presentation tailored for both Millennial and non-Millennial professionals as audience participants, you will discover empowering best practices, 'next practices,' and tangible take-a-ways on how the 'corporate melting pot' can leverage unique generational mentalities and expectations. You will learn how the arrival of the most hyper-connected, civic-minded and tech-savvy generation has impacted workplace culture and the way work will continue to get done.

Tailored version for marketing conference:

A new generation of creatives and marketers has emerged and officially become the majority workforce demographic. This population known as Generation Y, or 'THE Millennials,' is changing how marketing, communication and branding is being performed and accepted. Professionals that understand those strategies attracting the interest and attention of Generation Y will find better results in their marketing efforts. In this interactive presentation, you will discover empowering best practices, 'next practices,' and tangible take-a-ways on how to leverage and embrace unique generational mentalities and expectations. You will learn how the arrival of the most hyper-connected, civic-minded and tech-savvy generation has impacted how marketing and design gets done.

As you read my examples above, I hope the reaction that occurred to you was "I can do this! This makes sense!" Of course it does. Do not complicate the game. Just take action.

Using all the space you need - separate sheets if possible - write below sample sentences and phrases that describe your presentation:

Now that you have sample phrases and sentences - and keeping under 120 words - write below a draft of your presentation description:

I do not recommend continuing to the next section until you have a presentation description to work with. Flip back to previous pages and complete your presentation description if you have not yet done so.

Presentation Learning Outcomes

Learning outcomes are also called learning objectives. They are succinct statements that describe what the attendees will learn and take away through your presentation. Consider learning outcomes as articulated Call to Action statements. I am not always asked to provide learning outcomes but regardless, I always submit them. Having learning outcomes shows the organizer that you are clear on your objectives and action statements. My advice is to have learning outcomes ready. I recommend at least two learning outcomes but no more than four.

Below are a few learning outcomes from my Millennial program:

- *Learn about generational perspectives, both differing and similar, and how to embrace and leverage these unique mentalities.*
- *Discover what isn't being said and written about Generation Y that will lead to a new understanding about this new workforce majority and their needs.*
- *Leave with several 'Call to Action' and 'Next Practice' strategies for bridging the generations and building workforce synergy.*

Looking at your presentation description, write below sample learning outcomes. What will attendees learn and leave with?

I do not recommend continuing until you have between 2-4 learning outcomes.

Speaker Biography

Your speaker biography is extremely important. It must reflect your experience and the impact you have made both as a speaker and in the industry, or industries, you serve. Your speaker biography is not your speaker introduction. Your introduction is what someone reads to introduce you before speaking. It should be no more than 100 words and able to be read within 30 seconds. Your speaker biography can have more depth.

Look at it this way, your speaker biography is what attendees will *read* and your introduction is what attendees will *hear*. Most speakers are good with drafting a biography – shocker – because they enjoy writing about themselves. However, please be cautious about this. When I read a biography longer than the actual presentation description, I know am going to either be listening to, or coaching, someone with a very large ego.

Focus on the impact you have made more than the work you have done. Throw some humor in there. Be different. Add a fun fact. I have people come up to me all the time inquiring about information completely unrelated to my speech that they read in my biography. I learned early on that as long as I include the most relative experiences about my background for the industry I am speaking to, I should sprinkle some personality on there as well.

Below is an example of my speaker biography:

Dr. Kevin Snyder is a motivational speaker and author with a PASSION for helping individuals and organizations empower their teams and employees. Kevin has presented over 1,000 high-energy leadership presentations for a variety of organizations in all 50 states. Prior to becoming a sought-after speaker, he held a career in university Student Affairs and most recently served as a Dean of Students.

<u>FUN FACTS</u>: Kevin is author of several books, a TEDx speaker and organizer, an adjunct faculty member with the Center for Creative Leadership, a certified skydiver, scuba diver, sailing enthusiast, & game show winner on TV's 'The Price is Right!

<u>Keeping your speaker biography under 100 words, write a sample biography below</u>:

I do not recommend continuing until your speaker biography is complete. Flip back and complete your speaker biography.

Headshot Photo

Your headshot photo can make you appear less than professional or professional – which do you prefer? I have seen numerous speakers who just do not take this seriously. Your photo is likely what conference organizers/meeting planners will post online and on paper. You want your photo to represent you nicely and carry a professional aura. If you do have a headshot photo but it's more than a year old - get a new headshot. If you have gained, or lost, significant weight or have changed your hair color since your last photo - get a new headshot. If you are missing teeth, hair, a body part, etc. – get a new headshot. You get the point. Your headshot will make a statement about you before you even begin speaking. Make it look professional and, please, just look like your picture.

Headshots do not need to cost a lot of money. Ask around. Look on Facebook. Attend a charity silent auction and bid on photography. I attend charity events all the time and there is always a photographer package. You end up winning a professional headshot session for a fraction of the cost and you help charity. Respectfully, there are photographers everywhere. Talk to an emerging photographer and tell them you will credit their photography if they provide you with a headshot. For them it's free marketing. For you, it's a free headshot. Barter.

I have several headshots and I usually send a few samples to the conference organizers/meeting planners. I let them decide which photo works best for their group. Sometimes they use one for the website and another for the print or web app.

If you do not have a current headshot, where can you get one? Who can you call? I shared ideas with you above.

List resources below for what you will do to obtain a current headshot:

---

*I do not recommend continuing until you have listed
and contacted resources above to obtain a new headshot.
Flip back and complete the activity.*

Congratulations, you have come far. Since you have followed instructions and treated this chapter like a coaching session, I know you have not allowed yourself to advance until each section has been completed. You might be saying to yourself, "Well, I'll come back and finish this later. I want to get through the book first."

I understand your desire to get right to the Moneyball module – Module 3. However, there are aspects in Modules 3, 4, 5 that will not help you without having completed the foundations from Modules 1 and 2. You haven't graduated yet to Module 3 if you are still doing homework from Module 2. Please just trust me on this. More importantly, trust the process.

If any sections are not complete, please revisit them at this point.

Are You Ready For Your Speech?

No seriously, are you ready?

Now that you have your program title, description, learning outcomes, speaker biography and a headshot, you have the needed information to get booked as a speaker. Congratulations!

Let's assume that YOU receive an email right this second for a speaking engagement next week. Or perhaps you have a speaker friend who gets sick or has a family emergency last minute and needs YOU to take their keynote speaking spot TOMORROW. Are you ready? *No seriously, are you ready?*

I have had both these scenarios occur on multiple occasions for a variety of reasons. I flew across country on a day's notice to fill in for another keynote speaker whose parent unfortunately passed away. Because I felt ready to do the keynote and had the presentation information ready to launch, I got the gig and spin off referrals from it as well. When short term requests come in, that is where a speaker is tested. This is another reason to have your presentation ready to launch.

Now that you have what it takes to get a booking, let's focus on the presentation itself because we need to ensure you are getting referrals and spin off requests from each booking. The only way you will get those is by having such a powerful presentation that makes it impossible for an attendee to forget you. Throughout your presentation, you need attendees to be thinking, "This speaker is amazing. We have to bring them to our _____!" A presentation that does not lead to referrals and spin off opportunities means something didn't hit home in the presentation. Something needs to be worked on. I state this from experience both personally and in observing others.

People ask me all the time, "How did your presentation go in New York/Chicago/Atlanta/etc.?" I respond with, "Think it went pretty well. You should check my Twitter or Facebook page for some really impressive comments." Or better, I might say, "I woke up to some emails today from attendees that lead me to believe it went really, really well." Or even better, "I got five inquiries for speaking already. It must have gone really well!"

As you read in Module 1, the elements of an incredibly powerful keynote are **engagement, a powerful message, a memorable story and a call to action.** Each ingredient matters and provides its own secret sauce for an amazing speaking recipe. However, these elements are somewhat conceptual. What does a presentation outline actually look like? How is it structured? What should you include? Keep reading ... let's focus on designing a program that ensures a referral.

How To Design Your Presentation

Your presentation must be organized and crafted like a heartbeat. You want to organize the content - what I call the 'puzzle pieces' - around the emotions, sensations and interactive components that take your audience participants on an emotional and engaging 'ride' up and down, up and down. This will keep their attention whether you are speaking for six minutes or sixty. Incorporate everything you can - from audience laughter to empathy, from lecture to interaction, from hearing your words to watching a video. Your presentation should be organized to engage and connect with a different sense of perception - auditory, visual, kinesthetic. Just do NOT make them smell you.

I created a **Speaking Storyboard** to demonstrate how this heartbeat concept works. Take a few moments to look below at how I organize my presentation content and craft my presentation like a heartbeat. No one likes a monotone voice - so make sure your voice, your content and your delivery are not "monotone." Appeal to as many emotions as possible. See below:

As you design you presentation, ask yourself these questions about attendees:

When are they laughing?
When are they going to be emotional?
When are they moving?
When are they being reflective and writing something down?
When are they sharing with the person next to them?
When are they watching?
When are they listening?
When are they high-5'ing?

SPEAKING STORYBOARD

Time (Length/Total)	'Puzzle Piece' Title	Descriptors	Speaking Mechanics *
5/5	INTRO	Don't Stop Believin'	Moving
		Two Claps	Moving
		Three Concepts/Purpose	Listening
		Why this is important/What problem will we solve	Emotional
5/10	SHOW UP	80% of leadership is doing one(1) thing	Sharing
		Turn to your neighbor and Hi-5 !	Moving
		Quote: "Opportunities are never lost …."	Listening/Watching
15/25	THINK DIFFERENTLY	Success really looks like …	Listening
		Success Examples	Watching
		Roger Bannister	Listening/Emotional
		Nine Dots	Sharing
15/40	STORY	Etc.	Listening
		Etc.	Sharing
		Etc.	Emotional
		Etc.	Moving

* <u>Speaking Mechanics:</u>   <u>a</u>. Listening   <u>b</u>. Sharing   <u>c</u>. Emotional   <u>d</u>. Watching   <u>e</u>. Moving

You likely do not understand the content, or descriptors, in my storyboard. That's OK – you should not understand them because only I know my content. By having this one page, I have a clear mental picture of my keynote speech outline. What I encourage you to focus on is the speaking mechanics and how I ensure the 'puzzle pieces' of content vary in approach.

Important: Within the first sixty seconds of your presentation, your audience has already decided if they like you. Do what is necessary for them to be thinking, "Wow, this speaker is amazing ... funny ... inspiring ... different!" Otherwise, they will already be checking their phone – and perhaps their pulse - and you will have lost them. The "likeability factor" is imperative with your audience. They 'likely' have just come from another speaker they did NOT like for this exact reason.

The first 5 minutes of my presentations are simply fun - I go for immediate laughter and setting an energetic tone. We have plenty of time for content. My 'style' is to get them 'two-clapping' and singing 'Don't Stop Believin' ASAP. Observe sample videos on my website, www.KevinCSnyder.com, for examples. Point is to be likeable and immediately engaging.

I have reviewed presentation outlines from other speakers and find it extremely evident they lack organization and emotional variety. Unfortunately it's even more evident when they are on stage. Boring.

I was working with someone recently and I shared my storyboard concept with them. They replied, "I already have an outline. Look at this." When I did, their 'outline' looked more like a movie script. I thought to myself, "How in the world can they remember this content? Are they a famous actor and I just don't know about it?" I then asked them to show me specifically where in their outline the attendees would be laughing, doing something interactive, being reflective, watching or listening to a video or music. The response I received was silence and "deer-in-head-lights" appearance. We had a lot to work on. They were nowhere near ready. The fact they thought they were ready concerned me even more. Their movie script was also all about them talking. If I were an audience member, likeability would be zero.

As you develop your outline, you must also ensure your audience quickly knows where you are taking them. Once you are 'likeable' and have set a positive tone, make sure you are addressing the problem, or 'challenge,' that you will be helping the audience member solve. What is your point? Share it with them. Tell them how and why you can help. Otherwise, they will begin to wonder what your point is and why you are speaking. Once they begin to wonder, they begin to wander.

It is tough, if not nearly impossible, to get an audience back after you have lost them - another reason to appeal to a variety of senses to keep them engaged. Remember that you are there to help them solve a problem whether they know what that is yet or not. Some attendees, if not most, might be sitting in that chair listening to you because they have to be there or they are receiving credit in some form. Appeal to a variety of senses. Drop a statistic. Know their industry and share a relevant story. At the beginning, tell them what you plan on telling them. Tell them through your story. Then tell them what you just told them.

And remember, what you told them should help them solve a problem, or problems, and it should have a call to action.

Now that you have seen what my storyboard looks like, create your own on the next page. I have a different storyboard for each presentation. I move puzzle pieces around depending on length, audience, purpose and objective. Moreover, sometimes I enjoy just trying out new content. You can contact me or visit my website ('Resources' tab) to download additional storyboard templates.

SPEAKING STORYBOARD

Time (Length/Total)	'Puzzle Piece' Title	Descriptors	Speaking Mechanics *

* <u>Speaking Mechanics</u>: <u>a</u>. Listening   <u>b</u>. Sharing   <u>c</u>. Emotional   <u>d</u>. Watching   <u>e</u>. Moving

I do not recommend continuing until you have drafted your storyboard. Spend a few moments on this if you haven't done so already.

Presentation Aesthetics

What does your presentation actually look like? Are you using Keynote(Mac)/PowerPoint(Microsoft) or are you speaking with just a microphone? If you are using anything visual, please have someone review your slides before you incorporate them into your presentation. When you complete this book and earn your coaching call, I would be happy to share feedback with you myself on your presentation.

I constantly see horrible Keynote/PowerPoint presentations. I speak at a lot of conferences and I enjoy checking out other speakers. In fact, I would guesstimate that 80% of the presentations I see need quite a bit of work. I do not design presentations for my coaching clients but I would be happy to refer people who create slides professionally. Your investment in having someone help you will be priceless. An attendee knows when you put something together last minute or if it's done unskillfully – that attendee *could have been* your next speaking gig. The conference organizer/meeting planner is also someone you need to impress. They likely hold the gate key for additional presentations.

Your presentation audio/visual should complement your speaking. Anything coming out of your mouth should be written in a different way, if at all, on that slide. No bullet points. Font size at least 30. Aim for pictures rather than words. No more than 20 words per slide. Don't adhere to these recommendations and your attendees are squinting trying to read your slides and not listening to you. Do you really want them not paying attention to you and staring at a screen? Of course not.

I have sample PowerPoint presentations on my website you can view to get a flavor of my presentation style (click 'Resources' tab). I am commonly told my slides are engaging and visually appealing. I aim for pictures that portray the story I am sharing. It helps me and the attendee both. I also weave in 2-3 videos, add some music here and there and just keep it lively and fun. However, I am fully prepared to do my keynote presentation without visuals should my PowerPoint not be available.

Example: As I showed up to deliver a keynote presentation, I was told that their entire audio visual system was down. All they had for me were two handheld microphones. Prior to my arrival, and confirmed through 2 conversations, a contract and email, I was ensured that they would meet my AV request which included two projectors, two large screens and house sound for my interactive PowerPoint. I immediately had to adjust my content and plan for the worst. I couldn't even share my video of winning on *The Price Is Right* – my signature video. Well, I didn't feel bad for *me* – I felt bad for the attendees and even more for the conference planner. The fact nothing worked looked bad on the planner.

Point to the story is always be prepared in case your technology does not work. Expect it to fail and have a backup plan. If I wasn't prepared to present my program without any audio/visual it would have been a disaster. If I had not already envisioned something not working, which I do before every speech, then I would have looked like a chump on that stage with 1,000+ attendees in the audience.

Fast forward to the end of my keynote ... the representative for the audio visual company approached me with a handshake and a smile. The conference organizer was standing beside him as well. The representative said to me, "Of all the speakers I have ever seen, you have been the most engaging even without audio/visuals working. Best speaker I've seen. Good job today." My heart smiled. This experience was a test and luckily I passed. But it was not luck. I prepared for it. Technology problems occur frequently.

As Steve Jobs is quoted, "People who know their content don't need PowerPoint." Please, for the sake of the professional speaking business, know your speech. At some point in your speaking career, the projector will die, the computer will freeze up, your remote clicker will not respond to you, **and** your projector which was supposed to be there never showed up. (Note: notice I highlighted the word "**and**.")

Every single one of these situations have happened to me on multiple occasions. It's like skydiving. After so many jumps your parachute eventually will not open up and you will have to cut the cord to pull the reserve. Not fun. That's why I stopped skydiving after 12 jumps. Always be prepared for the worst case scenario.

With speaking you want to minimize the tools you need. Focus on your content, not your PowerPoint. When you need your slides, it more than shows. It suggests you are not professional and do not know your content. So never rely on PowerPoint or whatever medium you're using. If you need notes to speak, why? In that case, what you really need is simply more practice.

If you are getting paid thousands of dollars for keynote, or want to, the expectation is that you are an expert in your topic. Common sense? Well ...

common sense isn't so common sometimes. I have watched speakers fall on their face when their laptop died and they didn't have their crutch for reading the content. Painful to watch.

If you need notes at this point in your speaking journey, I understand. But that also means, with all due respect, you aren't ready for a paying gig – or at least an upper pay-tier speech yet. Moreover, I believe in God and I also believe in what we attract from the Universe. When you show both you are ready, that you don't need notes and you have practiced enough, an opportunity will come your way when least expected. You cannot fake professional speaking. You will get referrals because you are an incredible speaker with a well-prepared speech that has specific, thought-leading points.

Begin creating your actual presentation and consider using Keynote, PowerPoint or some other technology. You must plan on investing several hours of research and design on creating your presentation.

Practice

Let's assume you have your presentation ready now. Where can you practice until you feel ready to launch and really be found and PAID? What you do NOT want to do is practice on a group that could actually book you as a speaker. Even a Rotary group, who by the way books speakers each week, is not a group to practice on. You want to speak to them once you are ready to launch.

Even though they do not pay speakers, Rotary group members are business leaders who pay a decent chunk of money to be a member.

Your community is different than mine. You know your area best and are aware of resources available. I can help you identify more opportunities when we speak but consider these following groups:

- **Toastmasters:** They meet weekly and there are likely over a dozen different groups within a 20-mile radius from you meeting every day during all sorts of times. Start with 1 group and then consider joining two-three so you have several speaking opportunities each week. I am a member of three groups myself and I visit others when I travel. On some weeks I cannot attend due to travels but I try to attend meetings as often as possible. These are great groups that support speaker development and will help you improve your speech.
- **Meetup Groups:** Check out www.Meetup.com and search for groups related to speaking, leadership and networking. Just search and you'll find a variety of opportunities.
- **Networking Groups/Seminars:** Do a Google search for groups, contact your local Chamber of Commerce, look on Eventbrite, and just explore. You will find opportunities to speak and meet others who speak as well.
- **Facebook/Friend Inquiry:** Ask for referrals where you live. Ask friends, post on Facebook, call people. Do anything you can to find local groups and opportunities where you can speak, for fun, in order to practice.

Maximize

When you do find a practice opportunity to speak, maximize what you can glean from it. Videotape yourself and study the video. Audio record yourself and listen. If your video/audio is really good, and professional quality, you could even use it in your marketing. Count your "ahs" and "ums". Count how many laughs you receive. Practice new content. Keep old content fresh. Study your vocal inflection, your movements, and body language. Also, ask for feedback when you do speak. Create your own evaluation form and ask questions specific to the type of feedback you are looking for. You could even get some testimonials.

Example: When I was preparing for a new keynote, I leveraged all the above resources to practice new content, try out a new delivery style and hear feedback from those in the room. I videotaped myself and critiqued myself harshly, I watched the video on mute to study my body language and I listened to my presentation without watching. It is amazing to 'hear' communication that does not exist. If you have never watched yourself on video without audio, give it a try. You might need a stiff drink afterwards.

In my preparation I also created my own evaluation and asked each attendee to answer a few short questions on what they enjoyed most, what they felt was best, what they felt could have been improved and what could have been omitted. The feedback I received was priceless. Months later, when I delivered that keynote presentation at a direct marketing conference of over 2,000 attendees, I nailed it. I had both the confidence and content that made my keynote a winner. And as result, I received numerous spin offs and referral speaking engagements.

List the local resources below where you can find speaking opportunities to practice your content:

Module Review

In this module we have described, and you have created, your:

- ***One Page*, including your presentation title, description, learning outcomes, speaker biography and headshot picture,**
- **your presentation outline,**
- **what your presentation should look like aesthetically and**
- **tips for how to get practice opportunities.**

This was a chunk of a module. If you have completed all the reflective questions to your own satisfaction, then congratulations! You are ready for Module 3! However, if any portions are missing, I highly recommend you go back and complete them now. You will not be following this *PAID to SPEAK*™ system by speeding through this book. Remember, when you contact me to set up your complimentary coaching call, the first question I ask will be, "Did you complete each question in the book?" What you are reading is designed to be a coaching manual as well as a narrated version of my seminar. Coach yourself and complete the activities if you have not done so already! The checklist on the next page will help ensure you have completed each question.

"If you don't have time to do it now, when will you have time to do it again?"

MODULE 2 CHECKLIST

	YES	NO
I have my presentation title complete.	___	___
I have my description complete.	___	___
I have at least two learning outcomes complete.	___	___
I have my speaker biography complete.	___	___
I have an updated professional headshot.	___	___
I have completed my Speaker Storyboard.	___	___
I have my actual presentation ready.	___	___
I have practiced my presentation.	___	___
I have gotten feedback on my presentation.	___	___
I feel confident that I could present tomorrow.	___	___
I do not need any notes for my presentation.	___	___
I am ready for Chapter 3.	___	___

If you have checked 'YES' on all the items, proceed to Module 3!

Notes

Notes

NOTES

MODULE 3: FINDING & GETTING FOUND

It's not about who you know. It's more about who knows you!

Question: Do you find speaking engagements or do they find you?
Answer: Both.

I am consistently amazed at the variety of ways my speaking bookings originate. They have come from the associations I network with, from an attendee in the audience at a previous speaking event, from the spouse of an attendee who works with an organization needing a speaker, from one of the bureau's I work with, from a call for programs that I submit, from a fellow speaker referral, from my own marketing, from my social media, from sitting next to someone on a plane or at a coffee shop, from a blog I just wrote, from young professionals who saw me speak at their college and now work for a company needing a speaker and from my newsletter, just to name a few.

Point is you never know where your next gig will come from. You should always pursue an opportunity to speak. That means to be prepared and always ready to deliver. Do all you can to be visible so you can be found. That way when someone does need a speaker, you come to the forefront of their mind. It's not so much about *you* knowing who needs a speaker; rather, it's more about *them* knowing about you.

My marketing strategy is to be seen. Over 90% of my speaking comes from referral and usually that referral comes from somewhere unexpected as I previously described. Now I know to expect inquiries randomly so I strive to always be on top of my game. I do not invest much in marketing and frankly, my website could be better. I do not invest in pay-per-click advertising and I will not be suckered into marketing gimmicks.

Also, as I will share in the bonus chapter, "How to Write and Publish Your Book,' my **books** sell my speaking and my speaking sells my books. We will discuss the power of a book to leverage your speaking soon, but for right now just keep it in mind that a book can help you be found for speaking opportunities, can help you get the speaking gig and, most importantly, can help you double your fee. When people know about your book, they know about your speaking – and vice versa!

So the questions you need to focus on answering are:

"How can I find speaking opportunities?"
"How can I be seen?"
"Who are the people who book speakers and how can they find out about me?"

Now that you have a dynamic and engaging presentation loaded, it's time to aim and fire that shot at the appropriate target. What does that target look like though? Knowing the answer to that question is essential for your speaking success.

I always ask new speakers that I coach or mentor the following questions, "Who do you want to speak for? Do they belong to an industry? What type of person is sitting in that chair listening to you?"

Answers I commonly get are "Executives," "Anyone," "Colleges," "Uhmm," "Business Owners," "Uhmm," "Technology People" or "Not sure."

None of these answers will work. They are not focused enough. You need to have a specific vision for the type of organization and industry you want to be speaking for (Module 1). You have to be extremely clear on who you want listening to you and where you want to be speaking. Funnel your focus. The more specific you are, the more clear you will be on where to look. (I will ask you to list sample groups shortly.)

Your presentation can be suitable for a variety of groups, audiences and industries, but to get started focus on just one. Remember, chase one squirrel at a time.

Follow me for an example. Let's say you speak on topics of marketing. It should be obvious then that the speaking sandbox you want to play in is organizations within the marketing industry. Those could be marketing associations, networking groups, marketing agencies themselves, marketing departments within colleges, etc. I would recommend that you identify as many organizations as possible within this marketing niche – *if* marketing groups were your focus.

Although I speak to marketing groups on occasion, my speech topics are generally not tailored for the marketing industries. I am not as immediately familiar with all the types of marketing groups that exist as someone who actually worked, or spoke within, the marketing industry. However, I performed a Google search for "Marketing Organizations' and identified the following groups within 20 seconds:

American Marketing Association
Business Marketing Association
Interactive Marketing Association
The Marketing Association
Web Marketing Association
Mobile Marketing Association
Internet Marketing Association
Digital Marketing Association
Word of Mouth Marketing Association
Legal Marketing Association
Direct Marketing Association
Hospitality Sales and Marketing Association
Produce Marketing Association
Destination Marketing Association
American Wholesalers Marketing Association
International News Media Marketing Association
Multimedia Marketing Association
Etc.

I'm exhausted just thinking about all these different groups a speaker on the topic of marketing could focus on! This list alone could keep someone, i.e. YOU(!), fairly busy for prospective speaking opportunities. Every industry has dozens of associations that belong to it and book speakers for their events. The point I want to get across to you is that these groups were simple to find. And again, it is only a short list. I recommend you maintain an ongoing list of as many organizations and groups as you find in your speaking niche.

Also, from my search I mostly found association-level organizations. Of course you could identify marketing departments and companies singularly, and you should, but to get the best bang for your time investment, I recommend focusing on the associations first. Would you rather speak for one group independently or speak at the association meeting in front of 100 marketing professionals each representing a different company who could book you?

I hope you answered the latter. The great news is that this same principle, and process, applies broadly across all speaking niches.

Now comes the question of what to do with this list of groups and associations. What do *you* think you should do next?

Focusing on each association/group separately, I would identify local and statewide chapters and find out when and where they meet. Explore whether they have speakers at monthly/quarterly/annual meetings and conferences and what that selection process looks like. Attend their local meeting, network with their decision makers who bring in speakers, and begin building trust and likeability. Invest your time with them upfront and you'll likely be asked to speak. Asking to speak upfront might turn them off. It's a delicate dance of knowing who goes first. Start with cultivating the relationship. Be a giver, not a taker.

When you visit each local group, explore whether it is a group you should actually join as a member. If you speak to marketing organizations, keeping to my example, then why not join the local marketing association and network with other marketing professionals?

Example: I am shocked that more of my speaker colleagues do *not* think like this. For example, I became involved with and joined my local meeting planners organization (MPI). By the second meeting, I had been asked to lead a committee, had gotten to know all the leaders on the Executive Council and had been *asked* to keynote their Annual Meeting. I was the only speaker who attended the association's local chapter meeting. It made no sense to me why other speakers were not there at the same association meeting. In a way though, I am glad they weren't!

Back to you ...

Once you identify the local association/organization, look at how it is structured. If you found a local chapter in your community, for example, then this organization likely has numerous sister chapters within the state where you could speak. You could inquire immediately about speaking opportunities outside your local chapter through these sister chapters. If they know you are a member of the association, and if you use a bit of their "lingo" in your conversation and email messages, then your chances of getting booked are much better. They consider you one of them.

In addition to the numerous chapters within the state, there will be a statewide chapter, a regional chapter and a national/international chapter – all of which have annual meetings and conventions. Within one association alone, you could have your entire year of speaking all booked!

This model - system really - has been my *secret sauce* for not just finding opportunities and getting found, but also getting booked to speak – and PAID nicely. Let's put this model to work for you.

List as many industries, associations and organizations within your speaking niche:

If you are struggling with types of groups and industries, you are likely thinking too BIG. Think more specifically about the industry and professional title of the person you want to be speaking in front of. Who are they? What is their title? Are they a decision-maker? If not, who is their supervisor and what type of role would they be in? What is their formal position if listed on a business card? Who is sitting in that seat listening to you? With these questions in mind, go back and complete the preceding question to identify as many groups and industries as possible.

Now, select just **one** of these groups/industries and list below. Yes, just one:

If what you wrote down is an industry, identify the name of just one of the associations that it belongs to and write this association below:
(Note: at a later point you should repeat this process for each of the associations you can find within this industry)

Find the website for the association's local chapter and write below. Also, identify and write how often this chapter meets as well as when/where their next meeting is:

Now mark this date on your calendar and RSVP for the meeting. After you RSVP on their website, identify the leadership contacts for this group and send an email to the President, President Elect, and Membership Chair stating that you are a first-time guest and look forward to meeting them. That's it. Include nothing else in your initial email. Ensure that your message signature lists what you do and your website.

Be subtle. Be sweet. Chances are they will look at your website without you asking and notice your signature line indicating that you are a speaker. This drip approach works. Trust me. Trust this process.

When you attend that meeting, be sure to get there early and bring plenty of business cards. Meet the officers of the group/association and be sure to also introduce yourself to the VP Programs or whomever it is that books speakers. Just introduce yourself – no more – and tell them you enjoyed the speaker and commend them for the selection. Don't be eager on your first interaction.

Please, do not continue until you have completed the above tasks.

Congratulations, you will soon be connected and networking with dozens of professionals in the industry you desire to be booked for speaking! Let's not wait though. There still is work to be done.

As previously described, now you should further explore how this association is structured. Everything you need can be found on their website. Explore whether they have a statewide association – they likely do. Do they have chapters within the statewide association? When/Where is their state association conference? Do they have a regional sub-association and/or conference within the association? If so, list those details. Then, list when and where the national or international conference is being held.

By doing this homework you will quickly dissect not only how the association operates, but more importantly, all the opportunities where you could be booked as a speaker. This model is my bread and butter.

Follow this model recommendation and let it work for you. Don't follow it and you will likely not earn the results you desire.

I recommend answering the following questions as well:

<u>Does the association/organization you selected have a statewide association? If so - and they likely do - list the state association's name below</u>:

Looking at the website, how many chapters are within this statewide association? List the names of each chapter below:

By clicking on each chapter's website within the state association, you will want to identify which person at each chapter makes decisions on speakers. Likely their title will similar to a VP Programs or the President Elect.

For each chapter, write below the name and email for VP Programs/President Elect and indicate their chapter designation: *(Hopefully. You'll need more space to write so flip to the end of the module and list in the notes section.)*

Once you write this information, contact each of them and share your ***One Page*** as an attachment within a professional email. Your email could look like something as simple as this:

"Hello _____,
I speak to _____ organizations on topics of _____ and I help them to _____
_____.

Through your _____ website, I noticed that you are the appropriate contact who selects speakers for your meetings. I would be honored *to have you consider my engaging presentation titled, "_____." Attached is more information about the program which also lists some of my credentials. ... < if applicable, insert one more short sentence about you speaking to other groups, feedback received, etc. >*

I look forward to the opportunity of presenting to your group,

< your signature >

If you do not hear back within one week, make a phone call or send a very brief follow-up email and forward the prior email. If you do not hear back within another week, pick up the phone.

When/Where is this association's state conference?

List the contact person and deadline date for the call for programs at this conference?

Does this group/association have a regional sub-association and/or conference within the association itself? If so, list that name here along with date/location/call for programs deadline. Plan to submit a presentation.

List when and where this association's national or international conference is being held. Include the call for programs deadline date and plan to submit a presentation.

    I have followed this exact process with numerous industries and associations and it has worked each and every time. Once you complete the questions above for the industry you identified, select another industry/association and repeat this process. You will find that the majority of organizations follow a similar structure.

Speak For FREE?

Now, I know you are wondering, "OK, great, but do these organizations and associations PAY?"

Some chapters do and some do not. Conferences very likely DO. It depends on budgets and their philosophy on paying speakers. I'll discuss how to better monetize these opportunities in the next chapter, Module 4. For the purposes of this chapter though, you need to find the appropriate sandbox to FIND and BE FOUND. As an aspiring and emerging speaker you need to pursue every opportunity possible that puts you in front of the right people who might think, "Wow, this person would be a great speaker for our _____!"

You are much more likely to be invited to speak, and paid, if your reputation precedes you through referral from prior speaking at a few of the chapter-level groups. When they contact *you*, there's a fee. Furthermore, when you speak at these association meetings and conferences, you will be in front of dozens, if not hundreds, of different companies. I can think of no better marketing promotion for you than to do what you do in front of people who need and can benefit from your service. This is the genesis of PAID speaking. When your presentation is solid with a powerful Call to Action, you will receive referrals and inquiries. When those inquiries come in, then your fee kicks in. If the first one was free the second has the fee.

Question: Should you speak for free?
Answer: What do you think?

Speakers SPEAK! Plain and simple. You just need to play in the correct sandbox and learn how to be found by the groups you desire to speak to. Before you can get PAID to speak you need to learn how to be found and the best way to be found is to SPEAK! Which comes first, the speaking chicken or the speaking egg? Who cares?! Just SPEAK!

If 90% of my speaking business comes from referral, do you think I speak for FREE occasionally? Of course yes, but only when certain criteria are met. I'll go in more detail during our next chapter, Module 4.

Speaking To Colleges

I could write an entire book on college/university speaking and how to get booked – I probably will. There are over 5,000 colleges and universities in the United States alone. You have public and private institutions, colleges and universities, 2-year and 4-year institutions, proprietary institutions and even more.

From this point forward, when you read the word 'college' know that I am referring to all of the types of colleges and universities. Each one has numerous opportunities for speaking and most are at the PAID speaking level. College bookings typically pay $2500-$5000. Some gigs do not pay at all. You have to know where to look, who to **find** and who to **be found** by.

As I stated in the preface of this book, I started off as a college speaker. If you have not read the preface I encourage you to do so. It will shed light on how I evolved from "fun college speaker" to "professional motivational speaker." To date, I have spoken at over 500 colleges. On average my speaking fees have been $3500, some significantly more and some less. I encourage you to visit my website to see some of the colleges I've been honored to travel.

I understand colleges because that is where I started my professional career. I am also a former Dean of Students and I've taught as Adjunct faculty. I recognize that I have a significant advantage in the college speaking niche, just as you do in your own industry niche. If you have a desire to speak to colleges you should study and understand their structure. Speak with me. I can help ensure you understand.

Speaking to colleges will require a learning curve but do not get frustrated. Just focus. Once you understand how one college is structured and the types of groups that you could possibly be booked by, know that most colleges are structured in a similar way. Depending on the type of institution and size, there will be variation, but for the most part you will understand where to look.

Think back to when you or your children attended college. There was an Admissions Open House or campus tour. Once admitted, there was

Orientation. After Orientation there was Campus Activities Week. Depending on the types of organization(s) on campus, there were fraternity and sorority Greek Weeks, Student Government events, a variety of campus programs, student leadership conferences, activities sponsored by Resident Advisors and Hall Government, Homecoming events, Athletic events, guest speakers in classes, Lecture Series, Faculty/Staff events, Personal Development days, Parents Weekend, all sorts of Awareness Weeks which included topics such as 'Safe Spring Break Week' and 'Alcohol Awareness Week.' Toward the end of each semester, there were also banquets and leadership dinners of all types.

The groups above are a short list of just some of the collegiate organizations which have booked me to speak. I have developed a keynote presentation that appeals to many of these groups so it should be no surprise that my presentations have been successful. I am also proud to be on the roster for CAMPUSPEAK, a collegiate speakers bureau. They help represent me to these colleges but I also invest my time attending various student conferences which not only helps me stay in touch with my prospective audiences but also **be found** by them. (For more information about CAMPUSPEAK contact me or visit www.CAMPUSPEAK.com)

The question you need to ask yourself is, if interested in collegiate speaking, **"What is the type of collegiate group I want to speak to?"** Do you have a specific group in mind or do you feel that any type of group could book you?

If you feel that any type of group could book you, then I encourage you to re-read the beginning of this chapter. Colleges are very similar to the professional groups. You have to know the specific industry you want to speak to. Perhaps your message will appeal to several different college groups. Well, who are they?

Below are some sample groups you could consider:

- *Student Life Departments*
  (Campus Activities, Student Leadership, Student Government, Campus Activities Boards, Fraternities/Sororities, Peer Educators, etc.)
- *Academic Departments*
  (Business, Marketing, Communications, Education, Political Science, etc.)
- *Athletics*
- *Admissions*
- *Orientation Services*
- *Residential Life*
- *Faculty Development Groups*
- *Lecture Series*

Similar to researching associations, identifying the contact in each respective area is just a few clicks away on the college's and/or college association's website. Do some research on your own. Select a college and look at their website. You will quickly see that the type of group you desire to speak to has events listed throughout the year where you could be booked to speak! Once you know who these contacts are, I recommend you reach out to them and share your **One Page** – of course your **One Page** is tailored for the collegiate industry. If you are unsure how to tailor your presentation toward a collegiate group, then do research on the Internet to better understand the issues and challenges they face. You can also contact me. Also, since colleges are one of my expert niches, we can discuss this during your coaching call once you complete this book.

Once you identify the type of collegiate group you want to speak to, know that this group very likely has its own association as well, both professionally and for the students. Typically, the professional association is nationwide and they host an annual conference. The student conferences tend to be more regionally based. All of these conferences hire multiple speakers per event!

It is extremely important for you to consider which of the college groups you want to focus on. For example, let's assume you wanted to talk with collegiate women. After a quick Google search, I recommend you consider the following groups:

Panhellenic Associations (i.e. sororities)
National Association of Collegiate Women
American Association of Collegiate Women
University Women Centers
National Association of University Women
National Association of College Women
American Association for Women in Community Colleges
The American Collegiate Women's Association

Some of these groups are campus based at each college and some are more association based and only host regional and national conferences. After a bit of review and homework on your part, you can quickly determine where conferences are being hosted and who to contact for speaking opportunities. When you do speak at association conferences, you will likely be speaking in front of hundreds of campuses being represented, each with the potential of saying to themselves, "Wow, this speaker is great. We need to bring them to our campus!"

List below the college groups you feel your presentation is most suited for:

_____

Getting Referrals & Inquiries Yet?

Let's assume you have been speaking – you feel everywhere. You have been speaking for a variety of association groups at their local chapter meetings and for business networking groups. Perhaps you are already speaking at colleges. You are successful finding the opportunities but you are frustrated. **You aren't getting paid. Furthermore, referrals and inquiries are not coming in afterwards. What do you do?**

First, answer this question, why do *you* think that is? What feedback have you been getting from these previous speeches? Or have you been getting any feedback at all?

If you have been speaking consistently, 3-4 times per month or more but are not receiving referrals and inquiries, I would encourage you to review Modules 1 and 2 again. The content in these modules is where your answer lies.

You must reflect closely on what problem you are helping attendees solve, your Call to Action and the overall design of your presentation whether that be in content or delivery – or both. Something is likely missing or not powerful enough in the content you are sharing. Not receiving inquiries could also mean you are not speaking in front of decision makers or that you are not letting them know that this is your business of speaking. Let them know you speak for a living!

It is impossible for me to provide a proper prescription for you without an accurate diagnosis. I would need you to see your outline and watch you speak in action to identify further recommendations. Once again, contact me. Show me your Speaking Storyboard.

Ask for feedback from others as well. Invite people to watch you speak – ask for feedback. Befriend a fellow speaker and ask them to watch you speak – ask for feedback. Develop a relationship with an attendee who just saw you speak – ask for feedback. Record your next speech – ask yourself for feedback. Send me that video of you speaking – ask for feedback.

There are many ways to get feedback. If you do not ask, you will never know. If you choose not to ask, how has that approach been working for you? Chances are, with all due respect, it hasn't been working at all.

I receive feedback, and inquiries for future speaking engagements, every time I speak because I have my assistant follow up and ask for them. I also provide numerous ways for my audiences to share feedback with me and I will share how I do this later this Module and in Module 4.

Ask yourself again, why do you feel you have not been receiving inquiries and feedback on your previous speaking engagements? Do you need more practice? Is it your content? Is it your delivery style? Does your PowerPoint look like junk? Or perhaps the attendees you are speaking to are not decision makers?

Any of these questions above could be a factor explaining why the referrals and spin off inquiries are not flowing after you speak. Find out why. Get feedback. Continually improve.

<u>If referrals and inquiries are not coming in yet, why do *you* think that is? What do you think you need to do</u>?

Do You Keep In Touch?

Another reason inquiries and referrals may not be coming in is that you do not have a system for keeping in touch with attendees – whether they keep in touch with you or you keep in touch with them. This could be through social media (i.e. Twitter/Facebook/LinkedIn), your newsletter, a follow up email you send them, your newsletter and other means of communication.

Always be thinking about ways for an attendee to find you weeks, months or even years later. Attendees during your current and previous speaking engagements likely not have a speaker need tomorrow or next month, but they likely will sometime in the future. If you have a system of keeping in touch and you have built a solid list of contacts within your target industry, you will not be forgotten. Below are tips on how you can, and should, develop your system.

When I speak, I provide several ways for attendees to keep in touch with me. **First,** since Twitter is currently very popular, I add @KevinCSnyder to the bottom of every third PowerPoint slide in addition to a hashtag for the event/conference. As incentive to tweet, I announce a Twitter competition that rewards the top 'Tweeter' with a free book at the end of the presentation. At the conclusion of the event, during a video, I review the posts on the hashtag and follow those individuals. If I have my assistant with me, I have them count for me. After the presentation, I also ensure that I reply to direct messages and follow those individuals who have tweeted. Typically, if these individuals are not following me already by that time, they will follow me back when they are notified that I am following them. At the conclusion of my presentation, I also have a slide with all my social media information and encourage them to follow me to stay in touch. I have over 30,000 followers for this reason.

If you are not familiar with Twitter, you are missing incredible connection opportunities with your audience. I have booked speaking gigs through Twitter alone. You can visit YouTube for a tutorial on Twitter. Simply type in 'Twitter Tutorial' and you will be amazed.

Second, on the bottom of every handout, I list my contact information including email, social media usernames (which are all 'KevinCSnyder') and my website. You want to ensure they have your information and provide options for how attendees can keep in touch with you.

Third, on the bottom of my main handout, I have a statement that reads:

Write your name and email below to subscribe to my e-newsletter which will provide you with a complimentary copy of my book, 'Think Differently.'

Name: _____   Email: _____

If I do not use a handout, then I provide a quarterflier that mirrors this and also asks for testimonial feedback. I have found massive success with this process. Remember, you are giving away in order to receive. Attendees are less likely to give you their email or subscribe to your newsletter, for example, unless you are giving them something of perceived value such as your presentation slides, an activity, a free white paper, an eBook, subscription to your newsletter, etc. The key to building your list is by giving away something helpful and informative. Give to get. Below is a quarterflier sample:

FREE E-Book of Dr. Snyder's Best-Seller, '*Think Differently*!'

Text the word **KevinCSnyder** to **#22828** and you'll receive a complimentary copy!
(or write your email below and bring to front!)

Name: _____

Email: _____

I appreciate your feedback.
Submit a testimonial below!

What did you most enjoy hearing about today?
_____
_____
(please bring this card to front!)

Connect on Facebook/Twitter/LinkedIn!
'KevinCSnyder'
Kevin@KevinCSnyder.com

Fourth, when I do receive attendee names and emails from the handout or quarterflier, I connect with them on LinkedIn within 24 hours. This allows me to stay in touch with them via LinkedIn in perpetuity and it allows them to see my posts in the future. They are much more likely to accept my LinkedIn request if I connect quickly. Think about this approach and timeline from an attendee's perspective.

If they are hearing you at a conference, they likely also heard dozens of other speakers. Hopefully your presentation made an impact (Module 1 and 2) but with so much going on, expecting them to remember you on top of all the other speakers is not a good assumption. You are the one who needs to follow up – and quickly. When you do, include some point from your presentation so they connect you with your message. By doing so, you show professionalism and you stand out among the rest. From surprising experience, I would be willing to bet that most other speakers are not following up and none are following up as quickly as you. That is, unless both you and I are speaking at the same conference. In that case, I hope you beat me to it but the odds are against you! The key is to follow up quickly while their memory is fresh.

Fifth, within 24 hours I also send attendees whatever it was I promised to send, i.e. an eBook, article, video link, an activity, white paper, my presentation handout, or whatever it was that I promised. Waiting beyond this time window is destructive for you and your speaking brand. The longer you wait, the sooner they forget you and get back to being busy. You want to schedule time that same evening or early that next morning in order to specifically thank them for attending your session. Don't have time? Either make time or hire someone. Remember, this is what successful speakers do. It's business strategy.

In that follow-up message you also include the item you promised to send. If via email, that message could look like this**:**

"Thank you so much for attending yesterday's session on _____. It was a privilege speaking for you and I look forward to staying in touch!

As promised, I am sending you a free ecopy of my best-selling book, 'Think Differently To Achieve Success!' Simply <u>click here</u> to download your copy. If you enjoyed the presentation, you will enjoy this book – I guarantee it! If you would like for me to send this book to others, simply have them contact me or provide me with their email address.

I would like to stay in touch. Thank you and make it a PASSIONATE day!

< insert email signature here >

Important: On this first email, you do not want to promote yourself. You only want to give them what you promised. They will expect you to promote yourself. This is one of the very few times you do not want to meet their expectation! In fact, you should rarely promote yourself. Rather, let your speaking style and its content promote itself. When you share and post great content, your readers will appreciate YOU! Share CONTENT. Most speakers get this wrong.

List below how you plan on keeping in touch with attendees long after your presentation:

What do you plan on giving away in order to receive their contact information?

Share Your Content

As I briefly stated above, let your content be your brand. If you are not sharing content in a variety of media, then you are missing out on opportunities to build your following and connect with others. More importantly, you are missing out on an excellent strategy for attendees to remember you. You can share content through a variety of social media platforms - by blogging, replying and contributing to other blog postings, writing for an industry publication, sending a newsletter, etc.

By sharing content, you are earning free marketing. I would much rather invest 1-2 hours to write an article for an industry publication than to spend $500-$1,000 on advertising in that same magazine. In fact, if you 'share' your cards correctly, you could receive complimentary advertising space by writing an article/blog! Possibilities are numerous. Look for them.

I enjoy sharing relevant articles, commenting on other's articles and blog posts, sharing trending content, adding a funny video clip, attaching a motivational picture, quote, etc. I post at least a few times each week on LinkedIn, Twitter, Pinterest and Facebook. I also send out my e-newsletter every other week.

For example: you can subscribe to my newsletter by texting the word KEVINCSNYDER to #22828. Try it out as an example and you'll receive an autoreply confirmation. When I speak, I typically have 30-40% of my audience members text my number to receive my newsletter. My email platform is Constant Contact.

Even if you are starting from scratch right now, start somewhere. You will be glad you did later on. Or perhaps you already share content frequently. If you are already a frequent content generator, how can you take it to the next level? How can you brand yourself even better as an expert on a topic by sharing more content about it? Food for thought.

What is your strategy for sharing content and what media/platforms will you use?

Google Alerts

Google Alerts are a way to find speaking opportunities. You set up keywords and phrases, such as 'Marketing and Keynote Speaker Wanted,' and then anytime Google finds that announcement online, you receive an email – called an alert. Each alert is one particular keyword or phrase. The alert is up to you. You decide what the word or phrase is. You can set up as many different alerts as you wish. This strategy is simple, brilliant, and effective. I have received many speaking bookings through *Google Alerts*.

You should think about the popular words and phrases that will be used in the types of speaking announcements you are most interested in. You can edit, delete, or add alerts whenever you like. You also can dictate how often you desire to receive the alerts; daily via one email, separately for each alert, weekly, etc. I recommend a daily email for each alert so you can respond in a timely manner.

I also have my own name as a *Google Alert* – which I recommend you do as well. You want to know when your name pops up on the internet! Simply visit www.google.com/alerts to get started. Just be prepared to start receiving emails and opportunities.

List below the phrases and keywords that would best describe the speaking opportunities you are looking for:

Website

Do you have a website?

If *yes*, how would you rank your site on a scale of 1 to 10, 1 being "cr*p" and 10 being "amazing?" How would others rank your site? Unless you and others unanimously agree that your site is a solid 10, you have work to do. It's OK because I have work to do as well. I know my website could be better and I make changes to it monthly.

This segment will not focus on website creation, SEO, or what an ideal website should look like – that is not my forte - but you just need to determine whether your website is helping or hurting your speaking aspirations. What do you think?

If you do not have a website, it's beyond time. Although I have not focused on websites until now, it's time to recognize that the big players, meeting planners and conference organizers who PAY speakers significantly do look at websites and videos now more than ever. If you do not have a website, or do not have one that you are proud about, it's OK. You likely have numerous friends and contacts who do website design. Or contact me for a few resources to get your site made < $1,000 including videos and blog features. You do not need a website to get started speaking but you need a website to make big money.

All you need to focus on is the website content. You could generate significant fresh content for your website – or make revisions - within just a few days.

On your website, at minimum, you want to have an introduction/about page, keynote presentation(s) page, client summary or testimonials page, background/bio page, and a contact page. You will either want to weave pictures and videos in your, or have an additional link for those. You also will want to have a products page if you have products to sell or give away. Other features, like a blog or resources tab, would be additional recommendations.

I have both a products page and a resources page. I use my resources page to give out my free material referenced during presentations but you can only find it by visiting my products page first! Remember, give to receive!

I frequently hear about speakers who pay thousands of dollars for a website. This baffles me. Even after looking at their site, expecting to be "Wow'd," I am not. Why should websites be so expensive?

Assess your website objectively and get needed changes made immediately. It's time you have a website that you would rank at least a 7 or 8.

How would you rank your website on a scale of 1-10? What needs to be improved? What is missing?

Who is someone that can help you get your website up to speed? *(Contact me if I can help!)*

Module Review

In this module, you have learned:

- **how to find speaking opportunities and how to be found,**
- **how to dissect an association to find speaking opportunities,**
- **how to speak to college students,**
- **tips for building your list and staying in touch,**
- **how to build your brand through sharing and creating content,**
- **how to use *Google Alerts*,**
- **the importance of a website as it relates to PAID speaking.**

If you have completed all the reflective questions then congratulations! You are ready for Module 4, *Getting PAID*! However, if any portions are missing, I highly recommend you go back and complete them now. You will not be following this *PAID to SPEAK™* system by speeding through this book. When you contact me to set up your complimentary coaching call, remember the first question I will be asking you! The checklist on the next page will help ensure you have completed each question.

"If you don't have time to do it now, when will you have time to do it again?

MODULE 3 CHECKLIST

	YES	**NO**
I have identified several associations to target.	___	___
I have one specific association in mind.	___	___
I have reviewed their website and know how this association is structured.	___	___
I know when/where the local group meets.	___	___
I have RSVP'd for the next meeting.	___	___
I have contacted this group's leadership.	___	___
I have written down contacts for each chapter.	___	___

I have identified college groups I want to speak for   ____   ____
if applicable.

I have developed a system for keeping in touch.   ____   ____

I have begun a plan to share content.   ____   ____

I have set up several *Google Alerts*.   ____   ____

My website is a solid 8 on a 10-point scale.   ____   ____

*If you have checked 'YES' on all the items,
proceed to Module 4!*

NOTES

_____
_____
_____
_____
_____
_____
_____
_____
_____
_____
_____
_____
_____

NOTES

NOTES

_____
_____
_____
_____
_____
_____
_____
_____
_____

MODULE 4: GETTING PAID

If the first one is FREE, the second has the FEE!

This speaking motto has proven well for me many times over – *if the first one is free, the second has the fee!* What do I mean by this? Well, if I found an opportunity to speak but was told there was no speaker budget, then I might consider that *pro bono*, waived fee, speech as a marketing opportunity. I will not pass up an opportunity to speak as long as the speech is in front of my target audience and I am available within a reasonable amount of time. Referrals and spin off inquiries will result if my presentation delivers the impact that it should. When those second-hand inquiries come in, the fee kicks in as well. Make sense?

The challenge when agreeing to a *pro bono* booking is what you will do if a conflicting PAID opportunity comes along? For me, I do not agree to *pro bono* opportunities more than six months out. The likelihood of me being booked to speak is far too great. Furthermore, it is very, very bad business to cancel a speaking gig, paid or unpaid. However, sometimes the circumstances might be too tempting to pass up the opportunity – especially when you are starting out. If you do agree to speak without payment, I recommend providing a statement or clause in your contract that simply informs the meeting planner of this dilemma and how you will handle it. When they read this clause, they might change their mind and creatively find funds for you.

Moreover, there are many ways to monetize value and future gigs from a *pro bono* speech. Not only are you gaining experience and being visible so others know about you, but you also are gaining a new client for your client summary, building contacts, adding testimonials, getting video, selling books, selling your program (if available), receiving advertising space in their publication and more. Unless you are speaking for one particular company, you are in front of dozens, if not hundreds, of various organizations in a specific industry – your sandbox. Is that not what you want regardless if you are getting PAID? Answer should be "yes!"

I know speakers who are not willing to speak *pro bono* and they wonder why they are not getting referrals and desired results in their speaking business. Any successful speaker who says they do *not* speak for free is likely not telling the truth. Remember speakers SPEAK! It is impossible to get a referral for speaking if you aren't speaking. Remember that 90% of my speaking business comes from direct referral.

You probably are thinking, "OK, I agree, but I cannot speak for free all the time. I need to get PAID!"

You are exactly correct and I understand. This is where the association model approach I referenced in Module 3 comes into practice. What I love about associations is that once you get to the conference level, whether that be state/regional/national/international, they very likely pay and pay well. Think about it. They are charging a registration fee and a good conference organizer/meeting planner knows that a good speaker costs money. They have a budget for speakers! I have seen registration fees from $199-$999 for a one or two-day conference. Multiply that registration fee by 100 or 1,000+ attendees. Of course they have a speaker budget.

This is why speaking at organizational conferences is my bread and butter. I recommend you consider this approach as well.

Getting to this level doesn't happen overnight though. Speaking to at least one, if not a few, local association chapters of the association you want to get into will serve you well. Your reputation will proceed you and they will be contacting you because they know you are good and can deliver when it counts most – their annual meeting! Once you speak at their state or regional level and deliver well, then expect your next level to be at the national/international conference. Once you are in with an industry, you earn the speaker fee desired and you can continually increase it. For example, once I have keynoted 2 state conferences for a particular association, my speaking fee increases 25%.

Knowing that conferences, whether company specific or for an association, should be very lucrative, write below and remind yourself of the top three (3) conferences where you would like to speak:

When to Charge For a Speech?

"How do you know when to charge?

I have four simple criteria that help me quickly determine whether I have a fee, called a speaking honorarium, and if so, what that fee should be:

#1) Is this person contacting *me*? (as compared to me contacting them)

#2) Has this person seen me speak or been referred by someone who has seen me speak?

#3) Is this speaking opportunity at a conference where attendees pay to attend?

#4) Is this a new industry I want to explore?

If the answer is "yes" to the first three questions, then my proposal will require my standard speaking fee. If they are contacting me, have seen me speak (or referred by someone who has) and are charging a registration fee, then I have all the leverage. The only reason I would consider discounting a fee is if #4 were a factor, they were upfront about having a limited budget (and I confirmed this through my own homework) and I did not want to risk losing the speaking opportunity to get inside a new lucrative industry. Number #1-3 are no-brainers for me to keep my full fee.

Example: Several years ago I had spoken locally for a CPA group. I discounted my fee because they were upfront about not having the local budget available to pay my full honorarium and this was a new industry for me at the time. I agreed to speak but I ensured they understood they were getting a one-time discount and that my fee had to be kept confidential. The speaking gig went extremely well and the meeting planner just so happened to be the individual responsible for finding speakers at several other regional conferences later that year! They asked me to speak at 2 of those conferences and paid my full fee. Those opportunities put me in front of more than 500 CPAs throughout several states which led into further bookings as well.

During one of those regional conferences, I was approached about speaking at one particular state conference. They were upfront about not paying their speakers. However, knowing they met all three of my personal criteria for charging a fee, see #1-3 on prior page, I was not willing to waive my fee. Before responding back to them, I did my homework and looked online to find the website for this conference. I was pleased to read they were charging $499 per attendee!

I delicately responded back to their inquiry and thanked them for contacting me. I included my One Page, a link to my website and a sample video from the regional conference they had seen me present. I then indicated that I do my best to work within budgets; however, my normal daily speaking honorarium was $ < <u>my full fee</u> >. I also informed them that my honorarium included a full day of availability, additional breakout presentations, 50 complimentary copies of my book, and unlimited eBook downloads for all attendees.

I front-loaded value for them and stood out among the other speakers they were considering. They were asking me for a keynote presentation and the proposal they received back included options for a whole lot more. When they realized I could facilitate additional speaking sessions, it meant less work for them to find additional speakers. Also, by offering my complimentary eBook, this added value for attendees. The final result was that we negotiated a confidential price quite pleasing to me.

Below are some tips to maximize your speaking fee:

Tip #1: In your conversations and in your contracts, you must **state a confidentiality clause** about your speaking fee. Meeting planners and conference organizers talk, understandably and they should, but your fee is conditional on circumstances that *you* determine, not them. When your fee is confidential, only you and the organizer/planner know *what* and *if* you were paid. This is extremely important not only in your decision to discount any type of fee, but also for future speaking inquiries.

Tip #2: Have a daily fee. Whether you are speaking for 60 minutes or 6 hours, your day is booked. Unless you are speaking in town, it would be impossible for you to be somewhere else on the same day. Therefore, establish a daily fee for yourself and encourage the organizer/planner to utilize you as much as possible on that day. Organizers/Planners expect speakers to arrive and leave quickly. However, when you express interest in, and options for, maximizing your time, they appreciate that. This reflects positively on you as a professional speaker. I have been approached on numerous occasions by both attendees and organizers/planners and told they appreciate me being so visible before and after my keynote at a conference. Guess where that visibility leads to? You guessed right – more speaking bookings! We'll discuss this more in the next chapter, Module 5.

Tip #3: When you speak at conferences, **offer to facilitate extra sessions** as educational breakouts. Conference organizers/meeting planners love this even if there is not a need. Offering yourself to do more not only front loads your value but also makes them aware you have additional programs. Facilitating additional sessions is beneficial to you because it allows you to be in front of more people at the conference.

I cannot count how many times this strategy has worked for me and helped secure additional bookings. If my keynote presentation happens to be before the educational sessions, then I know those who attend the post-keynote session liked me, enjoyed my presentation, and are excellent prospects to hire me for speaking at their company. If my keynote presentation follows the breakout sessions, then I use the pre-keynote sessions to get my speaking juices flowing, know the attendees better and ask lots of questions. I'll incorporate as much as possible into my keynote presentation later on.

Tip #4: Offer something extra for attendees. As stated above, I offer complimentary copies of books with my full speaking honorarium. If I choose to discount my fee, then I include fewer books. What I love about the arrangement with my book printer is that I can tailor books for the group bringing me to speak. This allows me to offer a welcome letter on the inside page of the book.

This personal touch goes a long, long way for both the organizer/planner hiring me as well as the attendees. Having a personalized, tangible takeaway yields golden results later on. Providing a book is the equivalent of them taking you home and talking about you with others. We will talk more about the book in the BONUS section.

Which of these tips above can work best for you? Why?

List ideas for how you can add value to your speaking fee:

How Much to Charge: Setting Your Speaking Fee

You should now have a better understanding of when to charge, but how do you know *how much* to charge?

This is the moneyball question. It is also a tough question because part of the answer lies in a sense of self-worth. Of course we all want to be $20K speakers. But are we there yet? What do $5K-$15K speakers, let alone $20K speakers, do differently? The real question is, **how much does the industry you are speaking normally pay?** If you do not know, how can you find out?

Answering this questions requires a bit of homework and perhaps a bit of involvement on your part. One of the reasons I enjoy getting involved with certain industries/associations is because through committee meetings and Executive Boards I hear what/how they pay speakers. I hear it all. This is another reason to make your fee confidential. You want to minimize how many people know your fee.

<u>Pick one of the industries or associations you have previously targeted. How much do they typically pay a speaker</u>?

<u>If you do not know, how can you find out</u>?

Within the same week, I have spoken *pro bono*, another gig for $3,500 and another gig for $10,000. What determines fee can be industry and it can be psychology.

Industry: Let's say, for example, you want to speak at colleges. Well, you need to know that unless you are a celebrity or a mainstream comedian/actor/band, you likely will not be getting paid more than $5,000. In reality you can expect about $3,000. If you are sending your information to community colleges, Small Business Development Centers or small professional businesses, who *typically* have much smaller budgets, then do not expect $3,000. In fact, expect $300. You simply need to know parameters. I italicized *typically* for a reason because some of these groups can pay a higher fee. I am not suggesting you do not speak to groups with smaller budgets; instead, I am recommending that you be aware of budget limitations. Be aware and be realistic with yourself and understand what fee they can afford. Otherwise, you will constantly be frustrated. Do your homework.

While some professional organizations and industries simply do not have the budget, others commonly do – banking, health care, technology, legal, etc. The challenge isn't setting price with these groups; rather, it's knowing you have a presentation suitable for that industry. On a few rare occasions, I have been 'nickel and dimed' to speak for these groups individually – but not at conferences. Even with seemingly lucrative industries I encourage you to focus on conference keynote speaking – this is where the moneyball can be found.

Psychology: There is a psychology to the speaking business as it relates specifically to the amount of your speaking fee – and it fascinates me. Envision you have responded to an inquiry or you have submitted a "Call for Programs" to speak at a professional health care conference. (Note: a "Call for Programs" can also be called an "RFP" – "Request For Proposal"). Even though the meeting planner/conference organizer has contacted you, they will be comparing you with other speakers. As the person(s) responsible for speaker selection reviews the proposals, they narrow down to 5 different speakers. You're one of them. They are not sure whom to select though. Finally, it is identified that one speaker's fee is $10K and your fee is $3,500K. I can guarantee you that a thought held by all of them, and likely spoken, will be, "Well, the $3,500 speaker must not be as good. Let's go with _____ for $10K. We've budgeted for it."

This psychology may not make sense at first but think about the scenario from the organizer/planner perspective. Even with budget in mind, they are always looking for the best speaker. Your speaking fee will be a factor they consider and your amount will be perceived as the quality of you and your speech.

Example: I discounted a speech for a high school athletic conference several years back. They paid me $2,500 which I was pleased with because it was a huge conference, a new industry and it was in an exotic Caribbean location. Of course I would have wanted more, but I was available on the date they contacted me and it was less than a month away - meaning, the likelihood of me getting booked within 3 weeks was not probable. I agreed to do the gig. (Remember, speakers SPEAK!)

After the presentation, one of the attendees immediately approached me and we talked for several minutes. This attendee was a volunteer chaperone at the conference. I will never forget the exact words coming from her mouth, "I'd like to book you for my company. What is your corporate fee?"

I stood there like a deer in headlights. "Ughh, my corporate fee? Well … ughh." I felt like an idiot because I didn't know what to say. At that time, I had not done much corporate speaking.

She asked, "You do speak for corporate groups, don't you? What is your corporate fee?"

"Most certainly," I replied.

I should have replied, "Tell me more about your event." However, what I said was, "$6,500 is what corporate clients pay for my daily fee and that includes my availability all day, books, and a few other items." I threw that number out like a dart in the dark. I had no clue what the industry could afford to pay a speaker.

"$6,500?" she confirmed. "Send me a contract for $6,500 at this address," handing me her business card.

"I will have that contract to you by the end of tomorrow," I said.

"Excellent, thank you," she replied. "In the future though, you need to double that fee in the future because some people might not think you are that good based on your amount. Luckily I just saw you speak. I would have paid whatever you told me."

This situation is a perfect example of knowing your industry and the psychology that is attached to a speaking fee. Be prepared. Act as if you have been there. In this example, if I had told her my speaking fee was $3,500, she would have thought I wasn't good enough. If I offered $10,000 or more, she would have been happy paying the higher fee. I easily missed out on an extra $3,500 or more.

That will never happen again. Learn from me please. Know your industry.

You do not want to overprice yourself either though. This is a delicate balance and something that you and I should discuss one-on-one. I emphasize heavily to my client prospects, both in discussion and in proposal, that I do my best to work with budgets. That way they at least know there are options for wiggle room if needed. The ones who can pay do not ask for wiggle room though. They pay the full amount. Some speakers will disagree with me on this. That's fine because I likely will get their next speaking gig due to their inability to work with a client. This has happened on numerous occasions.

I have been surprised that other speakers seem very static with pricing. The organizer/planner feels the speaker will not budge on price and therefore won't even attempt a negotiation. This process is very similar to buying a home! A speaking honorarium can be negotiated so that both parties feel as though they win.

If I am available on a requested date, would I really want to turn down $6,500 even though I proposed $8,000? Or turn down $8,500 even though I offered $12,000? Of course not. (I might change this philosophy later on though! When I do, I'll write a new book.)

Be aware that your fee carries an assumption of credibility and quality. You want to know your industry and the common speaking parameters for honorariums. Do not undervalue yourself but don't overprice yourself either. Do your homework, be realistic and leave your ego at the door.

How much is your standard speaking fee/honorarium right now?

What do you envision this fee increasing to within a year?

What do you envision this fee increasing to within 3-5 years?

Proposals, Contracts and Invoices

You should create a separate document for your proposal, contract and invoice. I will be sharing samples with you on the next few pages. If you are one of my coaching clients, I am happy to review your drafts before you submit them to a potential client.

But first, let's review a typical process for how speaking gigs are booked:

Step 1: Speaking inquiry arrives.

Step 2: Response with questions/questionnaire and set up conference call.

Step 3: After call, **proposal** is submitted.

Step 4: After proposal terms and options agreed upon, **contract** and **invoice** submitted.

Step 5: 50% of your speaking fee is paid in advance. You receive the difference on the day you speak, if not before.

Sample Step 1: Speaking inquiry arrives.

Hi Kevin,

I received your information from my colleague _____. She had wonderful things to say about you and her experience in listening to your presentation at the _____. I was inquiring about having you speak at our Annual Business School Awards Symposium and Gala. The date is November 12th from 6-8 pm.

Please let me know if you are available and your fee to speak at this event.

Looking forward,

Kim

Sample Step 2: You respond with questions/questionnaire and set up conference call.

Hi Kim,
Great to hear from you! I work with Dr. Snyder as he travels to help him coordinate scheduling and logistics. Would you like to schedule a time this Thursday morning at 9:00am or 9:30am or 10:00am to speak with him? He's in the car during that time traveling.

It will be wonderful to learn more about your event and how he can tailor and deliver an engaging keynote on a topic related to one of his most popular topics --- workforce motivation! Attached are several of his leadership programs, but please know that he always tailors his content after speaking with you.

<u>*In preparation for the phone call, a few questions that he'll likely ask:*</u>

Do you have a theme for this year's event? Also, could you share last year's conference website?
Are you interested in him facilitating additional breakout sessions on top of the keynote presentation?
What are three learning objectives/outcomes for Kevin's presentation that you would like for your audiences leave with?
What is your speaker budget for this event?

Anything else you can provide would be extremely helpful in preparation for his phone call. He can reach you directly and his number will be #919-633-9931.

Thank you!

~ Sarah Edwards, M.Ed.
Logistics Coordinator for Speaker/Author Dr. Kevin Snyder
Info@InspirActiveSolutions.com

After we collect initial information from the inquiry, a phone conversation is scheduled to further identify the objectives and conditions surrounding the speaking opportunity. I want to learn as much about them as possible. I need to know whether they are charging attendees, audience size, outcomes they expect, which presentation(s) they are most interested in, facts about their industry, etc. I also want to know how they heard about me.

Some of this information I learn by simply asking and some I find through my own homework before the conversation even takes place. You want to appear solid, standard and professional but also excited about the opportunity. By the end of your conversation, you must know exactly what they are looking for.

Tip: It's always best to keep them talking. The best phrase that works in my discussions is, "Tell me more about ..."

At some point in the conversation, they will either ask you about your speaking fee or you need to ask them what their speaker budget is. Hopefully you already have a sense of their speaker budget and what types of speakers they have hired in the past. If you have done your homework, you'll know.

I prefer to be the one who brings up speaking fee. Discussions on fee are usually addressing the elephant in the room. Within 10-15 minutes on the phone, that topic has to be discussed. If I am bringing up fee, I keep it simple by asking, "What is your speaker budget for this event?" Even if they have already responded to the question about fee via email, I ask again for confirmation.

I then shut up and listen. Whatever next comes out of their mouth will determine what my proposal looks like. I have lost gigs because I didn't know a prospective client's budget before submitting a proposal and overpriced myself. I have also lost thousands of dollars because I underpriced myself. Point is, it is imperative to know budget. Just ask.

Tip: When the fee issue is being discussed, I tell them I have a daily fee with a range based on several options. The proposal they will receive after the phone call will provide those options which could include:

- *Availability of additional breakout sessions*
- *Purchasing quantities of book(s)*
- *Including personalized book(s)*
    (note: I consistently double my speaking fee with a customized book. Contact me for details.)
- *Including eBook downloads*
- *Discounting daily fee with conditions, if necessary*
- *Including travel or having travel as additional*

The key is for the prospective client to know that your proposal will have options. It could be discounted options if they indicated your fee was too high or it could include additional 'up selling' options if they agreed to your fee upfront. I recommend that your proposal have options for them to consider. Always leave room for Jello.

I sometimes take off the additional breakout session options and/or books if needed to discount my keynote speaking fee. They are fine with this and it makes them feel they are still getting what they wanted from me. After the contract is signed, I likely will throw the session options back in anyway and possibly even include the books. Whether they pay for the books or not, it's additional marketing for my speaking.

Note: as we'll discuss in the BONUS book section, my books cost me < $5.50 each. Why not give 50 books out when I'm getting PAID $6,500+?

Sample Step 3: After call, **proposal** is submitted.

Each proposal is unique based on the conversation you had with the prospective client. I share templates and review proposals with my coaching clients. Share your draft with me and I'll be happy to review.

Motivational Training Seminars &
Keynote Leadership Presentations

PROPOSAL: _____, Orkin

Dear _____,

It was a pleasure speaking with you recently! Thank you for the inquiry to make a presentation for Orkin Pest Control!

I am honored to have made over 1,000 motivational keynote presentations in all 50 states for a wide variety of organizations and conferences. Each presentation is customized for the audience and industry I am speaking to. Talking in further detail with you will help me tailor the presentation to meet your needs and ensure that the content provides powerful call-to-action takeaways. With that said, I am confident about delivering an incredibly engaging, dynamic and motivational presentation that will inspire excitement for your team throughout the year!

If viewing this proposal on your computer, please click here to review my client summary, here for testimonials, or visit my website at www.KevinCSnyder.com. Most commonly, I'm asked to keynote for business workshops and conferences seeking dynamic and thought-leading speakers. By selecting me for a keynote presentation, you'll receive much more value than any other speaker can provide – **I guarantee!**

For example:

- *My engaging delivery style that keeps audience attention and enthusiasm.*
- *I have the business background and experience required to relate to your audience.*
- *Options for full day availability. Use me for additional presentations/keynote sessions!*
- *I customize each presentation based on your objectives. No "cookie-cutter" presentations!*
- *I will modify my presentation and title to fit your theme, if available.*
- *Option for 100 complimentary autographed books on site for attendees! More can be purchased.*
- *Option for UNLIMITED book e-copies for all attendees!*
- *My fees are all-inclusive. One fee = low maintenance!*

On the second attachment, I am providing you with a few keynote presentations to consider with descriptions and learning outcomes. Based on what you are looking for, I can blend presentations together. As I've previously emphasized, I always customize.

I am also confirming current availability _____, 2015. That date has a "Hold" for you; however to confirm and block this date for your event, a contract is required. Thank you.

NEXT PAGE PLEASE

Customized keynote presentations · Over 1,000 keynotes in all 50 states · www.KevinCSnyder.com

Speaking Honorarium

Due to travel logistics, customized preparation, delivery, supplies and follow up, speaking bookings normally have a daily honorarium fee ranging from $5,500 - $8,500. Due to your organization being relatively local, I am happy to significantly discount this honorarium price. Based on our previous conversation, below you will find discounted options. Please keep these discounted options confidential.

Revised Option #1:
One hour presentation on _____,2015. With insight from you, this presentation will be customized to meet your objectives, theme (if available) and any other desires.
Orkin price: $_____.00 *(Normally $4,500/day + travel)*

Revised Option #2:
In addition to option #1, this option also includes 80 personalized and autographed copies of my best-selling book, *"Think Differently to Achieve Success!"* - normally $12.99/book. On the book's inside front cover, I will add a welcome message from you and the Orkin logo. Additionally, this option includes unlimited e-book downloads - normally $6.99/book. Download quantities are unlimited and can be shared with anyone throughout your entire Orkin organization on that day. If this option is selected, I will need the welcome message and logo by Friday, September 11, 2015.
Orkin price: $_____.00 *(Normally $6,500)*

Revised Option #3:
In addition to option #2, this option includes video recording and editing so that segments of the keynote presentation can be shared with your team of employees throughout the year via video. I will hire a local production team to professionally record the entire presentation (2 cameras) and then edit the footage based on the time stamps you select. Each separate segment will be professionally edited with intros/outros and returned to you through both YouTube and as raw video files. This is an ideal opportunity to continue the conversation and further anchoring the themed message of **Think Differently** throughout the year.
Orkin price: $_____.00 *(Normally $7,500)*

To view videos, testimonials from prior meeting planners, as well as a client summary, please visit my website @ www.KevinCSnyder.com. A recent 2015 client provided the following feedback:

> "Dr. Snyder was one of the best keynote speakers our organization has ever booked! His presentation was interactive, tailored to our audience, and most of all, it was extremely entertaining! Whether you are seeking a speaker for your corporate organization, you will be impressed and inspired! Highly recommended!"
> ~Jason R. Pike Senior Vice President, BancorpSouth

Thank you _____!

-Kevin Snyder, Ed.D.
Kevin@KevinCSnyder.com
www.KevinCSnyder.com
919-633-9931

After submitting the proposal, ask for confirmation they received it and indicate that your availability likely will change. This will sprinkle on a sense of urgency for them to make a decision quickly. In my proposals, and contracts, I emphasize that opportunities arise on a daily basis and that I make decisions based on contract signage. This process is similar to buying a house!

Within a few days or weeks, you might need to follow up. If so, simply inquire via email or phone. You might need to nudge them and let them know another inquiry has arrived and you need to hear back from them by the end of the week.

If they decide not to go forward with you as the speaker, find out why. That information and reasoning will help you in the future. Thinking positive though, let's envision the scenario that they select you as the speaker for their event and go with option #2. Option #2 includes your keynote and books! Woot! Congratulations. Now all you need to do is follow up with a contract and invoice … and perhaps write a book!

Sample Step 4: After proposal terms and options agreed upon, **contract** and **invoice** are submitted.

After your proposal arrangements are agreed upon, the contract outlines and confirms details. Nothing should be a surprise and expectations should be transparently clear. You include everything from date and location, to speaking session(s) titles, when deadline dates are, fee payments, additional add-on's, travel, confidentiality, etc.

My contract is two pages and has been vetted by attorneys. I keep it simple to be readable and clear for planners and organizers. If the meeting planner/organizer has their own contract, read it carefully and make sure you understand it and agree to the terms. <u>Important</u>: Still submit your own contract to them as well! It will ensure you get PAID when you expect to be, not when they tell you.

I have reviewed contracts before that are not in my best interests as a speaker. In fact, I recently reviewed a contract that contained a clause literally stating they would only pay me if they had sufficient funds to pay me. I struck through that clause and had them sign *my* contract which included a 50% deposit.

A sample contract can be viewed on the next page and I am happy to share additional contract templates with you as well as review your first contract.

Contract for Speaking Engagements, Products & Services

Speaker: Kevin C. Snyder
Company Name: Kevin C. Snyder Leadership Programs
Employer ID #: _____
Address: P.O. Box 219, Oriental, NC 28571
Phone: Direct: 919-633-9931
Email: Kevin@kevincsnyder.com
www.kevincsnyder.com

Contracting Entity: _____

_____

The Speaker agrees to design and implement a motivational keynote presentation for the _____ on October 8, 2015. The presentation will be customized with the "Think Differently" theme and from previous conversations and agreement between Speaker and Contracting Entity. Content will be focused on a variety of leadership principles such as empowerment, sales motivation, creativity, passion, goal setting and other leadership development concepts.

Speaker also agrees to full day availability on October 8th as well as 80 customized books containing the _____ logo and message located on the inside front cover.

As has already been provided, the Contracting Entity will work with the Speaker to help him understand prior to his arrival what his schedule will entail, what the desired outcomes of each aspect of the schedule are, a description of any room that will be utilized, and the number of people expected for the program. The Speaker and Contracting Entity have discussed and agree to A/V technical equipment needed for the presentation which will be a microphone (lavalier/lapel preferred), a projector, screen and sound for the laptop. Note: the Speaker has a Toshiba laptop.

The Speaker and Contracting Entity agree to an all-inclusive speaking fee of $_____.00 which includes the 80 customized copies of 'Think Differently to Achieve Success." Travel expenses will be the responsibility of the Speaker. There will be no other exchange or billed expenses related to this date unless otherwise agreed by all parties.

A balance of $ _____.00 is due by _____ to confirm booking and availability. The remaining balance of $ _____.00 will be due prior to presentation date or onsite the day of event. Preferred payment type is check.

Total Contract Price Agreement: $_____.00

If paying with check, please make checks payable to: Kevin Snyder

If mailing checks, please send checks to following address: P.O. Box 219, Oriental, NC 28571

The Speaker agrees to be photographed, recorded, and/or videotaped for future non-commercial uses within the same organization. If photos and/or videos are captured, Speaker asks for copies.

Fully agreed to, binded, and executed by signing below. Thank you!

Speaker: _____   Date: _____
                Kevin C. Snyder

Contracting Entity: _____   Date: _____

Upon acceptance of this Agreement, please sign at the space indicated and return a signed copy. THANK YOU for this wonderful opportunity!

Invoices: I send the invoice along with a contract. The invoice is the bill statement. An invoice is what most of the companies need to process payment. The invoice is different than a contract for this reason.

My invoices now require 50% deposit upfront to confirm booking agreement. Most groups will pay this. In fact, it makes you appear more professional. It shows skin in the game. If they cancel on you, it is their dime and not yours. Of course, you hold yourself to the line as well, even if a higher-paying gig comes through for that same day.

Example: I learned the hard way once and once is all I need. I had a discounted speaking gig come through but we didn't have a contract signed. This was a client I had done some previous work with and expected all circumstances to be covered due to our prior positive relationship. Two months after agreeing to be their keynote speaker, I had another gig inquiry come through at full price. I had to turn it down though, because I was already committed to the first and they were a recurring client. However, to make a long story short, one week before the gig was to take place, they canceled on me – "not enough registrants for the conference." I missed out on not only 1 gig, but 2! I share this with you as proof that you should always have a contract, collect a deposit and have criteria for when you discount a speaking fee.

Tip: When something negative happens, don't ever allow it to happen again.

Sample Step 5: 50% of your speaking fee is paid in advance.

A sample invoice can be viewed below:

Invoice for Speaking Engagements, Products, Coaching & Consulting Services

From:
Kevin Snyder Leadership Programs
P.O. Box 219
Oriental, NC 28571

Date: _____, 2015
Invoice #: 235

Invoice to:

Description of Services	Amount
This agreement is made by and between Kevin Snyder and _____ for a motivational presentation customized based on previous conversation(s). Eighty(80) customized books are also included in this fee.	_____

NAME: _____

TOPIC: "Think Differently"

EVENT DATE: _____, 2015

Deposit amount to confirm booking: $_____
Remaining balance due on or before presentation date: $_____
TOTAL AMOUNT: $_____

Notes/Comments:

* THANK YOU!

* Deposit payment due by _____.

* Payments can be made via check or through credit card. Full payment is appreciated in advance of presentation date; however balance payment can also be accepted onsite. Any payments after 30 days of presentation will be assessed 10% due to administrative follow up.

* If paying with check, please make check payable to:
    Kevin Snyder

* Please mail deposit check and remaining balance check to following address:
    Kevin Snyder, P.O. Box 219, Oriental, NC 28571

Let's review the process one final time.

Step 1: Speaking inquiry arrives. *

Step 2: Response with questions/questionnaire and set up conference call.

Step 3: After call, **proposal** is submitted.

Step4: After proposal terms and options agreed upon, **contract** and **invoice** submitted.

Step 5: 50% of your speaking fee is paid in advance. You receive the difference on the day you speak, if not before.

If you followed the Modules, you should have inquiries arriving by this point! Responding to inquiries is easy ... it's getting inquiries that can be time intensive and frustrating! You will though by applying the PAID to SPEAK system!

Proposals, contracts and invoices ... you will want all these documents ready as soon as possible. Not having them ready will cause you delay in responding to inquiries and confirming your speaking opportunities. I also feel that not having the documents ready is akin to the Universe knowing you are not yet ready for the opportunities to come. Similar to what you learned in Module/Chapter 2, be ready for an opportunity. Let the Universe know you are expecting the inquiry.

True Story: Earlier this year I was contacted at 4:17pm by a meeting planner to speak at a major conference next year. For some odd reason, she needed a contract and invoice by 5:00pm that day! I didn't ask too many questions when she told me upfront, "We'll pay your full fee. I need it today."

<u>Do you have templates for your speaking proposal, contract and invoice</u>? <u>If so, write 'YES' below. If 'NO' develop them before moving on. Contact me for templates</u>:

Module Review

In this module, we have described in detail the importance of:
- **speaking *pro bono*,**
- **how to graduate to larger speaking gigs,**
- **criteria for establishing your speaking fee,**
- **understanding what your target industry can afford,**
- **the psychology of your speaking fee,**
- **the process from inquiry to proposal to contract/invoice, and**
- **having sample proposal, contract and invoice templates.**

If you have completed all the reflective questions then congratulations! You are ready for Module 5, *Getting PAID Again*! However, if any portions are missing, I highly recommend you go back and complete them now. You will not be following this *PAID to SPEAK*™ system by speeding through this book. When you contact me to set up your complimentary coaching call, remember the first question I will be asking you!

The checklist on the next page will help ensure you have completed each question.

"If you don't have time to do it now, when will you have time to do it?

MODULE 4 CHECKLIST

	YES	NO
I understand the importance of speaking *pro bono*.	____	____
I embrace the power of speaking locally in order to speak with larger groups later.	____	____
I understand recommended criteria for when to charge.	____	____
I have set my own criteria for when to charge.	____	____
I understand tips for maximizing speaking fee and adding value.	____	____
I have a better understanding of what to charge.	____	____
I have done homework and know what my target industry(ies) can afford.	____	____
I understand how speaking fees can be impacted by industry and psychological factors.	____	____
I understand the difference in a proposal, contract and invoice.	____	____
I have a template for proposals, contracts & invoices.	____	____

*If you have checked 'YES' on all the items,
proceed to Module 5!*

NOTES

NOTES

NOTES

Module 5
Getting PAID Again

"Repetition is the mother of skill."
~ Anthony Robbins

Are you anxious and excited yet to start getting PAID to SPEAK? If you have followed the modules appropriately, you should be busy responding to inquiries and following up on speaking leads!

If you have held yourself accountable to complete each section but are not feeling momentum or clarity, ask yourself "Why?" Why do you feel stuck? When we touch base I will help you. Whatever you do, do not STOP! You might actually be two feet from gold. The phone call or email you've been longing for is just around the corner. You are likely less stuck than you feel. I share this from experience working with others.

Speaking professionally is a business. Just like any business where customers purchase a product, the office doors just being open does not mean people will walk in and buy product. The store owner must provide a service or product that people want, need and know about. The owner must also give a potential customer a reason for walking in. In this scenario, you are the store owner. You must do the same consistently for your speaking business. If people are going to hire you for speaking, they must want, need and know about you.

You have accomplished so much by reading and completing the guiding questions in this book. Let's revisit what you now understand about the business of speaking that you likely did not know before.

<u>You</u>:
- *have a good understanding of your speaking aspirations.*
- *have reflected on your speaking parameters and limitations.*
- *understand how your speech can help an organization and its people solve problems and challenges they are facing.*
- *know what differentiates you as a speaker.*
- *have developed a powerful Call to Action in your speech.*
- *created an engaging program that keeps attendees involved.*
- *know what industries are most applicable for your topic.*
- *have identified several associations in those industries.*
- *know when and where these associations meet.*
- *are attending events in the near future to network in these groups.*
- *know how to submit programs at the state/national/international conferences.*
- *are excited and have strategies about ways to connect and keep in touch with professionals in those industries.*

- *understand what your ideal association/industry typically pays speakers.*
- *know how not to under/overprice yourself.*
- *are clear with how to frontload value and negotiate/maximize price.*
- *have a proposal, contract and invoice ready to launch!*
- *are ready for that first check!*

Your System for Speaking

Despite what you may have heard, there is not just one step in the secret to success. Success is the result of a system. Similarly, getting booked and PAID, for speaking is the result of a **consistent system being applied.** Many factors matter. If even one aspect of the system is missing then the whole system suffers - like spokes on a bicycle wheel. If even one spoke is too long or too short, the entire wheel suffers. The result will be a rough ride. I hope you have identified what your spokes are so that your 'wheel' spins smoothly and quickly.

What I have shared in this book should help you identify a personalized system. Your approach, based on your speaking niche and delivery style, might be different than mine – it will need to be. The importance of a system is that you have one and you make it your own. Then, you apply that system over and over becoming more successful each and every time.

In this chapter I am going to share a collection of tips, recommendations and lessons learned that have helped me develop my overall system. Some of the items I have never told anyone. I've learned the hard way on many occasions and I also have learned from watching others learn 'harder.' Either way, these lessons learned are teachable moments. Just as I learned from others, you can learn from the mistakes I have made. As you progress, you will make your own lessons as well. Share those with me and I'll include that wisdom in the next book!

If the speaking business was easy, there would a lot more speakers out there. Sometimes I think there are already too many. However, as long as speakers are making a powerful and authentic impact, then that's quite a bit of empowerment and positive influence being applied in this world.

The reality is that the speaking business is just that - a business. You have to treat it as such. **If you treat speaking as a hobby, then you will have a hobby income. Treat speaking as a business and you will have a business income.** If you have read this far and have completed the reflective questions, you have demonstrated that you plan to treat your speaking as a business. Expect those type of results.

<u>Are you planning to treat your speaking as a hobby or as a business</u>? <u>Write which one below</u>:

There will be times you want to give up or question yourself. That's OK. Expect to feel that way so you are not surprised. It's during these times you need to make yourself a participant in your own speech. What advice would you give yourself? Walk your talk. Do what you encourage others to do. It's an interesting role play scenario.

Example: A few years after writing my first book, *Think Differently*, I went through a tough time personally for a few weeks – my dog had been killed, I had a bad breakup, my real estate investments were beginning to go upside down, I had a sciatic nerve issue in my back ... you get the point. After listening to me gripe and complain for over an hour, a good friend of mine asked me, "Didn't you write a book about how to deal with this 'stuff?'"

Wow, this set me straight pretty quickly. It's tough to be a motivational speaker when you are not feeling motivated yourself. So at the end of the day, you have to walk your talk. Do as you say in your presentation.

Prime your own motivational pump. No one is going to do it for you. You know that. The only way you are going to maximize your success is by doing those things that most people will *not* do. And *that* is why you will be successful. When other people quit, you do not. When other people get frustrated and doubt themselves, you do not. You march on and push through the frustration because you have a guiding vision for speaking. It is only a matter of time before that speaking opportunity comes through. Prime your own pump!

<u>What advice would you give yourself right now about speaking</u>?

How Bad Do You Want It?

If you are going to be successful, you need to possess the same desire for SPEAKING that you do for breathing. When you want something bad enough, you'll do seemingly crazy things in order to manifest it in your life.

Example: A few years ago, I thought I had purchased a flight for one of my speaking engagements. The day before the engagement, I went looking through my email files for a copy of the flight itinerary. I could not find my reservation anywhere. After a few phone calls to the airline, I realized my mistake. I had never actually purchased the flight!

Buying the flight the day before was going to cost me half the amount of the speaking engagement itself. Canceling the gig flashed through my mind but I immediately recognized that was not the right thing to do. My only real options were to purchase the sumo-expensive flight or rent a car and drive ½ way across the United States. If I drove, I would save considerable money but it was a 16-hour drive and … I would need to leave immediately.

I looked at my dog sitting next to me. If he could talk he would have said, "Stupid Dad. Just stupid." I literally said to my dog, "We're going on a road trip boy."

I packed my bags, rented a car, and drove 16 hours through the night for that speaking gig. I got there 2 hours before the presentation, did the keynote, took an hour powernap afterward, and then hit the road and drove 16 hours back. In two days, I drove over 2,000 miles. The car rental agent was not happy with me when I returned the car. He asked, "Where in the he*l did you go!?"

Yes, this trip was crazy. I didn't tell anyone about this random act of craziness until writing this book. At first I was extremely embarrassed about my mistake. Now I realize that this experience was actually a test of my hunger for speaking. I passed.

I have had a few other late night and early morning drives but nothing as ridiculous as the story I just shared with you. One thing for certain is that I have never missed booking a plane reservation since. Lesson learned.

On a scale of 1-10, 1 being 'not so much' and 10 being 'I'm starving,' how hungry are you to speak?

Circle what you just wrote above!

_____

Surround Yourself With Support

The reality is that some people will question your pursuit for speaking. Some close to you might even doubt you to your face. It is crucial that you surround yourself with people who believe in you and support your speaking aspirations. There are doubters and haters everywhere unfortunately. Perhaps your motivation for them is not through a speech, but rather in being a walking testimony about the importance of living a dream and stepping outside of a comfort zone to try something new. Don't talk to them about speaking; rather, show them the results of having a dream for something. When you don't feel supported contact me. It will be my privilege to pump you up and remind you that you can be as successful as YOU want to be. What matters is what you believe.

I do recognize though that if you are married with three children and considering quitting your job to launch into speaking, your spouse might question how the bills will get paid. That is understandable. You don't have to quit your job. You can still pursue speaking by taking one step at a time, like I did, and setting the proper parameters for your speaking. Begin with the end in mind and follow your passionate vision. It'll bring a new life and energy to your world. As Zig Ziglar said, "When you have passion for something, you'll eventually find a way to make it happen."

If you have complicated circumstances, and everyone does in some fashion, treat your strategy for speaking like planting a garden. Your thoughts and desires are seeds. You plant those seeds in the right soil, sunlight and then you water them daily. Those seeds grow into plants over a period of time and ultimately they bear fruit. As this metaphor demonstrates, you truly do reap what you sow.

Plant your speaking seeds and nurture them with your 'system' of care. Over time you will be fascinated in what grows. The fruit you will bear will be determined by how you nurture the seeds and surround them in the right type of environment you create. Be patient and ask for support and patience from those around you. You need their support more than anything. Understand if they have concerns about your new journey and why. Strive to communicate your plan and strategy so they have confidence in why you will be working so hard. Once they understand, they'll be on your side. If you feel like they are not on your side, chances are they need to better understand your 'why' and also your 'plan.'

<u>Write the names of people close to you who you feel will, or already do, support your pursuit of speaking</u>:

I recommend you contact these individuals and let them know you appreciate their support in advance. Let them know you might rely on them for support in the future. Be grateful to them early on. You'll receive that back tenfold. Surround and embrace yourself in their support.

However, do not be surprised that some people close to you may not understand or support you as you might expect – or hope. What's most important is what you believe. However, if the person not giving you full support is your spouse, for example, then it's in your best interests to fully understand their concerns. It's likely an issue of communication. Remember, plants do not grow overnight. Neither will your speaking. But your speaking will grow and could further grow beyond your wildest expectations.

<u>Write the names of people close to you that you feel might challenge you or not understand your pursuit in speaking:</u>

<u>Why do you feel these individuals will not understand or support you</u>?

There will be times when you get advice from others you may not like. Expect it. People will give you unwarranted criticism, tell you what to do and make comments that you do not agree with. During these times, I want you to remind yourself of one thing - **consider the source.**

True Story: Not too long ago, a coaching client called me with a few questions about speaking. I felt we had a positive breakthrough in our prior weekly call and I was looking forward to hearing progress. After hearing a few of his questions, I was surprised. I asked, "Who have you been talking to since our last coaching session?"

There was silence on the phone so I repeated my question.

"What do you mean?" he asked finally.

In a delicate tone, "I mean, someone has gotten into your head and made you doubt yourself. You know the answers to these questions. What makes you doubt yourself right now?"

He said, "Well, I was talking to _____ and they were telling me something different."

I paused. I had invested quite a bit of time with this person and I was quite surprised he allowed himself to get stumped by a naysayer who didn't even speak for a living. He was now questioning the strategy we had developed together for his speaking success.

I kept silent.

"Are you still there," he said.

"I am," I said. "Look, you have come tremendously far since we have been working together. I am proud of you. The questions you just asked me though have answers you already know. Why question yourself because of what one person says?"

"Well, again, this other person just gave me some other recommendations," he said.

I replied, "With all due respect, _____ is not a speaker. They have no clue how to make a dime in the speaking business. Please, consider the source when you talk with other people. What this other person told you is not something I would recommend."

Moral of the story – consider the source when you get feedback and advice. If you receive feedback from someone about speaking who is not a speaker, what do YOU think you should do?

Consider the source. Contact me if you have a question or idea.

Please acknowledge below that you will consider the source when receiving feedback. Simply write "YES" below as a commitment:

Showing Appreciation To Clients

How do you plan to thank you clients for hiring you to speak? When they invest in you are you showing your appreciation? If so, how?

Regardless of my honorarium amount, I always send an immediate thank you via email to all those involved with booking me to speak. They have a message waiting for them the next morning. Additionally, within 2-3 days I send a hand-written thank you card. I make my own personalized quote cards which are an excellent branding tactic. I have received pictures via email and text from clients that show my thank you cards framed and placed on desks and walls. My point to you is, send a hand-written thank you.

For speaking bookings where at least a significant portion of my fee is paid, I send an edible arrangement. I'll typically invest $75-$100 on a nice arrangement without blinking an eye. It's a business expense plus their entire office will likely be grazing on it all day long and asking, "Who sent the arrangement?" Hopefully the answer will be, "The incredible speaker we just booked!" See how that works? Showing appreciation and gratitude makes an impact.

What are some of your ideas to show appreciation to your clients after they book you to speak?

Keeping In Touch

How are you keeping in touch? Or are you? This goes back to Module 3 and developing a system for staying in touch. If you do not have a system by now, why not? There are plenty of resources out there to help you. Some cost money and some are free. I highly, highly recommend you develop a system for staying in touch not only with attendees who opt-in to receive your information, but also with your clients and prospective clients.

Note: Never, ever, ever send unsolicited emails or newsletters to people who do not opt-in and give you permission to contact them. This is a HUGE 'no-no' and will place you on their unprofessional list. You'd be better off not sending them anything than to send them information they didn't ask for.

Example: Several years ago I received a speaking booking directly as a result from sending a newsletter to opt-in subscribers. It had been months since I had sent anything and I was doing a poor job of keeping in touch at the time. The email I received read:

> *Kevin! I remember seeing you present at a conference over two years ago. I'm sorry I couldn't remember your name, but I remember you speaking about The Price Is Right! Our company just announced they are looking for speakers at our upcoming conference and ironically I just received your newsletter. Can you please send me your availability for March 4 and program information/fees? Thank you!*

Wow, I love emails like this for three reasons. First, this example proves a point that meeting planners and executives may not need a speaker tomorrow, this month or even this year. However, when they do need a speaker and you have kept in touch, you will be on their mind. Second, did you catch the plural word 'fees?' It wasn't a typo. In this scenario, my full fee was paid. Third, you can see how my criterion for establishing speaking fees works. In this example, the person making the inquiry was contacting me and had seen me before.

You also want to have a system for tracking speaking leads. For me, I do this with a simple email folder. I simply file leads and prospective speaking opportunities in my 'Leads' email folder. I then make it a point to look inside this folder every 2-3 weeks to make follow ups. I'm sure there is a better 'system' for this, but this process works for me.

What is, or will be, your system for keeping in touch?

What is, or will be, your system for tracking speaking leads?

Referrals

When referrals are made on your behalf it is a beautiful thing. "Wow," you might be thinking. "People are helping me speak!" Of course this feels great. However, when was the last time *you* made a referral for someone *else*? Referrals are a two-way street. Remember, give to get.

You might be thinking, "Why would I want to refer someone else and give away business?" You're not giving away business. You make referrals for other speakers to clients who have already booked you to speak. Since they just brought you to speak, they likely will not be bringing you in again for 2-3 years, regardless of how awesome you were. Speakers are rotated. Why not ensure that rotation stays in the family. When you refer others, what do you think happens afterward? They usually refer right back to you ... it's a beautiful thing. This referral network doesn't always work the way it should because not everyone is a giver.

True Story: A few years back I received three speaking inquiries within the same month where I was not available. I hated missing these opportunities but I referred each of these inquiries to one particular speaker colleague who I knew could deliver a powerfully engaging keynote. Within one month, I had referred my colleague over $10,000 in business.

You would have thought that I might have received a nice thank you card, a bottle of wine, a gift card, or perhaps even a nicer gesture of appreciation. I hand delivered him over $10K in speaking gigs.

Well, what I did receive was ... nothing. In fact, the only 'thing' I ever received from this person was a text message stating "Thanks!"

I didn't refer these speaking opportunities with the expectation to get anything back. However, it is an unspoken gesture of professionalism to provide recognition when others help you get business. This person is lucky I didn't require a commission or have the contract go through me. To this date, I have never received a referral from the person referenced in this example. I also have never referred him again.

<u>Who are other speakers you would be willing to give referrals</u>?

Create a Checklist

Without a checklist you will forget something important when you need it the most. Learn from me.

I have forgotten my laptop charger, my wireless remote clicker, my introduction, my travel itinerary, contact information for the meeting planner, my cell phone charger, etc. If you do not have a checklist yet, create one. Once you forget something, like me, you'll develop a checklist.

I have printed copies of my checklist and I place them on top of my suitcase before each and every trip. I also have a checklist for all the pre-speech details. I write these items in my calendar so I do not forget. Sample on the next page:

SPEAKER CHECKLIST: DO NOT FORGET!!

Pre-Event Communication
- Review and follow script for 'Final Happy Call' 1-2 weeks out.
- Reminder/Update call 2 days before.
- Get copy of finalized agenda/schedule.

- Inquire about updates/changes. Review copy of agenda/schedule. Confirm logistics, room set-up, handouts being provided, AV needs, ppt, arrival time, sound check, lavalier/lapel mic?
- Will someone be picking me up from airport? (if required)
- Will room set-up include tables, moveable chairs, etc.?
- Will participants have pens?
- Music playing before I am introduced?
- Confirm length of presentation time. When is hard stop?
- Cell phone of point of contact: _____
- Location address: _____
- Time for sound check: _____
- Name of AV tech: _____

Packing The Bag – confirm day before
- License and flight itinerary, car itinerary and hotel itinerary
- Back-up debit/credit card
- Directions to venue location
- $150 cash
- Laptop & Battery Charger
- Wireless remote clicker and extra batteries
- HDMI cable and sound cord
- Pens & stapler
- Referral slips, handout copy and 2 copies of introduction
- USB (w/ ppt saved); also email to myself and upload to Google Drive
- Bag of prop items (TPIR shirt, hamster wheel, rubberbands, etc.)
- Video recorder and tripod; ensure space is available on recorder & charged.
- Books and Square processing for books (have $40 in cash for change)
- CD with music.

Type your AV/Tech Requirements

Set yourself up for success, not failure. Your meeting planner needs to know everything you need for your speech. Having it in a document makes you low maintenance and also professional. Create your sheet now! My sample is below:

AV/Technical Requirements for Keynote Presentations

Speaker, Kevin Snyder, will bring with him:
- Toshiba laptop (Non Mac)

Contracting Entity is asked to provide:
- Projector with VGA connection cord for connection from laptop to projector(s)
- Projection screen (for audiences above 300, 2 screens are recommended)
- AV cord that runs sound from laptop to house sound system (for video sound in presentation)
- Monitor in front of stage facing Speaker, if possible, so Speaker can see presentation rather than look behind. (Note: Kevin does not need PowerPoint; rather, to ensure he knows what audience is seeing!)
- Lavalier microphone for Kevin
- Additional handheld microphone (for audience participation)
- Skirted table on-stage
- One chair on-stage
- Assistance for providing handouts to audience members upon arrival

For questions, please call #919-633-9931 or email Kevin@KevinCSnyder.com.

With Passion,

~ Kevin

Dr. Kevin C. Snyder   *   Tailored workshops/Keynotes/Coaching   *   www.KevinCSnyder.com   *   @KevinCSnyder

Offer to Create Event Promo

Usually an event planner doesn't need it, but I offer to create an event flier or marketing piece for them to share with attendees. By having it in an attachment, they can forward it along via email. They could also copy and paste on the event website, if available, and distribute however they'd like.

I provide marketing promo videos as well. These are more complicated but very effective. Consider how you can help promote the event where you are speaking. Even if the planner doesn't take you up on your offer, they will appreciate you for it. And, they'll remember you for it as well. Sample on the next page:

About Kevin Snyder, Ed.D.

Speaker, TCC, September 17!

Dr. Kevin Snyder is a multi-author and motivational speaker with a passion for helping individuals *think differently* to live their dreams. As a keynote speaker, Kevin has traveled and presented over 1,000 programs in all 50 states and numerous countries. He has visited over 300 colleges and universities speaking and consulting with faculty, staff and students. Kevin will be speaking here at TCC on Thursday, September 17!

Kevin is a student affairs professional and has worked for 2-year, 4-year, public and private colleges and universities. He has experience in academic advising, orientation, counseling, student activities, fraternity and sorority affairs, residence life and much more. Most recently, he served as the Dean of Students for High Point University.

He earned a doctorate in Educational Leadership from the University of Central Florida. His research was focused on retention and persistence factors for first-generation college students who transferred from 2-year to 4-year institutions. Portions of his presentation to TCC faculty on September 17th will be focused on his research findings and how they apply to the TCC community.

A few interesting *fun facts* about Kevin:
- He recently sold his house in NC to achieve a dream of living on a sailboat.
- Kevin presented a TED talk titled "The Ripple Effect" receiving 400,000+ views
- He's also traveled the world on a college program called Semester at Sea.
- Kevin's a former game show winner on television's 'The Price is Right!'

Meet Kevin and join us for his presentation on May 17th!

Location: Building 201
Time: 2:00pm
Who: TCC Faculty & Staff

PAID To $PEAK!™: How to Become a Professional Speaker   www.PAIDToSPEAK.biz   www.KevinCSnyder.com

Carry Your Speaker Introduction With You

Your introduction sets the tone for your speech. Make sure you are introduced the way you want to be. Carry copies of your introduction with you regardless if you have previously sent the planner an introduction. With so much on their mind, they will likely forget it anyways.

Remember that whomever is introducing you is not a speaker. They are likely the boring CEO or Executive Director who has no clue how to engage an audience. Take control of your introduction by having it with you. I have been introduced so many horrible ways. The worst introductions were always when I wasn't prepared by having my own with me. Learn from me. Samples below:

SPEAKER INTRODUCTION (students)

Dr. Kevin Snyder is a 2-time author and *recovering* motivational speaker with a passion for helping others find theirs. As a keynote speaker, Kevin has traveled and presented over 1,000 programs in all 50 states and numerous countries.

Kevin was anything but motivated though growing up. He struggled, enduring challenges ranging from poor academics to depression … even being arrested. He was a near dropout on many occasions until he finally made important life changing decisions.

His presentation today … is about those changes. More importantly, it's about YOU and 3 leadership principles that will make you unstoppable in whatever you set your mind to.

A few fun facts before we get started about Kevin:
He recently sold his house in North Carolina to live a dream of living on a sailboat. Kevin's also traveled the world on a college program called Semester at Sea. He's a former Dean of Students, a dog lover, a certified skydiver, and best of all … he's a former game show winner on television's 'The Price is Right!'

Give a warm welcome to our keynote speaker, Dr. Kevin Snyder!!

SPEAKER INTRODUCTION (youth)

Dr. Kevin Snyder is a 5-time author and *recovering* motivational speaker with a passion for helping others find theirs. Kevin is also the Founder of *Empower YOUth!*, a leadership program for teenagers and educators throughout the United States. As a keynote speaker, Kevin has traveled and presented over 1,000 programs in all 50 states and numerous countries.

Kevin was anything but motivated as a teenager though. He struggled, enduring challenges ranging from poor academics to depression … even being arrested. He was a near dropout on many occasions until he finally made important life changing decisions.

His presentation today … is about those changes. More importantly, it's about YOU and the impact you make in the lives of students.

A few fun facts before we get started about Kevin:
He recently sold his house in North Carolina to live a dream of living on a sailboat. Kevin's also traveled the world on a college program called Semester at Sea. He's a dog lover, a certified skydiver, scuba diver and best of all … he's a former game show winner on television's 'The Price is Right!'

Give a warm welcome to our keynote speaker, Dr. Kevin Snyder!!

SPEAKER INTRODUCTION (corporate)

Dr. Kevin Snyder is a motivational speaker and author with a PASSION for helping individuals and organizations empower their teams, employees and workforce culture. He has spoken for over 1,000 audiences in all 50 states including dozens of _____.

With his research on workforce motivation, background as a Dean of Students, leading young professional organizations and speaking to over 300 colleges and universities, Snyder is an expert on Generation Y – better known as the Millennials!

Prior professional speaking, Kevin held a career in university Student Affairs and most recently served as the Dean of Students for High Point University. His Masters and Doctorate degrees were both earned in Educational Leadership.

Snyder has also written several books including the newly released '*Empower Your Employees!*', has been a featured speaker for TEDx, and is a former game show winner on 'The Price is Right!'

Develop a Fee Sheet

You'll know when you are ready to develop a sheet that lists all your speaking fees and options. When planners see a fee sheet, like below, it will set you apart. Assumptions will be made that this isn't your first speaking rodeo.

I share my fee sheet mostly with planners. Planners need to have a document on file for their budget. As I hope you notice, I emphasize that I consider working within budgets for certain groups.

Speaking Honorariums for Engagements

Organization Type *	Type of Event/Service **	Length (use Dr. Snyder for more than just a keynote!) ***	Daily Fee (includes full day of availability) ****
Corporations, Gov't and/or Associations	Keynote presentation at annual/regional meeting or conference, teambuilding workshop/retreat, recognition/training event, or serving as emcee	Ideal keynote length is 45 minutes-75 minutes; workshops 60-90 minutes; for conferences, recommend keynote + educational sessions	Domestic: $8,500.00 International: $12,500
Non-profit Organizations	Keynote presentation at annual/regional meeting or conference, board retreat, teambuilding workshop, recognition/training event, or serving as emcee	Ideal keynote length is 45 minutes-75 minutes; workshops 60-90 minutes; for conferences, recommend keynote + educational sessions	$4,500.00
	Emcee, auctioneer or charity fundraising initiative	1-3 hours	$3,000; 20% donated back to charity
K-12 Organizations (High school and middle school)	Keynote presentation for student conferences, school assemblies, teacher workshops, district training meetings & parent events; ideal for Title I and IX initiatives	Ideal assembly length is 45-55 minutes; recommend assembly (1-3) followed by teacher workshop and parent event (full day availability)	$6,500
College/University	Conference keynotes/Leadership Training/Retreats/Orientation/ Fraternity and Sorority Life/Staff & Faculty/Open House/Career Fairs	Ideal keynote length is 45 minutes-75 minutes; workshops 60-90 minutes; for conferences, recommend keynote + educational sessions	$4,500

Dr. Kevin C. Snyder · Speaker/Author · Over 1,000 Presentations in all 50 states · Tailored Workshops & Keynotes · www.KevinCSnyder.com

NOTES & CONSIDERATIONS

- In the spirit of a 'low maintenance' philosophy, speaking honorarium fees are **all inclusive** and include the following:
    - Travel (exception – Int'l travel; when Int'l, travel costs paid by organization booking Dr. Snyder)
    - All supplies, copies, handouts, etc.
    - A full day of availability for Dr. Snyder; utilize him for one or more keynote presentations, educational breakout sessions, additional organization, etc.
    - Complimentary unlimited E-book copies of Dr. Snyder's three books: 'Empower Your Employees', 'Think Differently,' and 'Leading The Way: Stories of Inspiration and Leadership."
    - Fifty (50) autographed, hard-copy books
    - Additional books available for 30% discount
    - Option for your organizations logo and customized welcome message to be placed on first page of book interior

DR. KEVIN SNYDER

- To secure booking, a signed contract and 50% deposit due. Remaining balance due within two(2) weeks of event or check provided onsite. No dates are held without signed contract or deposit.

THANK YOU for considering Dr. Snyder at your event!

Hand-Written Thank You's

In addition to my quote cards, I also send a more formal hand-written thank you to my clients. This simple gesture goes a long way. I will include my letter, my quote card, a few autographed copies of my book and anything else I think would capture my appreciation.

Dear Jason,

I can't thank you enough for the opportunity to speak and be a part of your special event with BancorpSouth. It was an honor to be involved and I was extremely impressed with all the logistics you coordinated. From beginning to end, you were incredible to work with.

Feedback is always something I value & I sincerely appreciate hearing after a presentation. If you'd like to share, or if attendees shared, any comments, takeaways, testimonials, etc. – anything – I'd love to hear those thoughts. You can email me directly or I'm happy to find time to talk.

I look forward to staying in touch. If you think of any ways I can help or support you by any means, please do not hesitate to contact me. I'm more than happy to be involved with a future event or leadership/training initiative with your group or any other organization you are involved. It would be a privilege to work with you once again.

In the meantime, #LivetheDream!

With Passion,

~ Kevin

Dr. Kevin C. Snyder * Tailored workshops/Keynotes/Coaching * www.KevinCSnyder.com * @KevinCSnyder

Set Realistic Expectations

I have worked with aspiring speakers who quickly become frustrated because they spent a few hours sending out emails but never received a response. They expected immediately to get 3-5 speaking bookings a month. They expected to be immediately paid $5000 a speech but became frustrated with speaking *pro bono* or at a discounted rate. They became frustrated when referrals and inquiries were not following a presentation.

We discussed this in Module 3 and 4. You now know that you must implement a system approach for both FINDING opportunities and being FOUND. Speakers SPEAK. No one can refer you for speaking if they have not seen you speak. Moreover, no one can inquire with you for speaking if they do not know about you.

It is a slippery slope when you begin to doubt yourself. Do not listen to that negative mental chatter trying to convince you that you will never be PAID to speak. Do not allow yourself to become frustrated. Remind yourself you are so close. You just need to have the proper expectations within a realistic timeframe. Neither expect results too quickly nor too far out. For whatever it is worth, I am confident you will achieve success much more quickly than I did. What took me 14 years should only take you less than 4 months if you apply what you read and learned from this book.

Important: Even the most famous speakers have teams of full-time speaker bureaus and administrative and marketing professionals making phone calls, sending emails and paying prime marketing dollars to coordinate and promote their speaking, books and seminars. I will not drop any names –

well maybe just a few: John Maxell, Wayne Dyer, Tony Robbins, Les Brown and Success Seminars.

This should be an 'aha' moment for you. It is crucial that you recognize even the highest paid speakers must advertise and lay rubber to the road somehow. They do not sit back and wait. Rather, they pay people to advertise and help them be found. In fact, think of the last time you became aware of a seminar or speaker presentation. Without needing to know what type of event it was, I would be willing to wager that the only reason you knew about that speaker or event is because someone was paid to promote it! Even for successful speakers and seminars, it takes a village and a lot of work to be successful.

Note: I am a huge fan of John Maxwell, Wayne Dyer, Tony Robbins, Les Brown and Success Seminars. I would not pick on names of people or groups if I didn't already respect them. I name them to point an example for you simply prove my point. Apply your system and work hard. Set realistic expectations.

What are your speaking expectations?

Write down the date you expect to earn your first PAID speaking opportunity:

How much do you envision being PAID?

The Best Athletes Have Coaches

I have written this book with you in mind. I hope that my writing style has felt both conversational and supportive. My sincere intent was for you to feel empowered with practical examples, stories and tips from the road. Unlike other books about professional speaking, I did not want to simply tell you what to do. Rather, I aimed to help you understand the power of a system that outlines what you need to develop and apply.

Now that you are close to finishing this book, it is imperative that you find someone who can continue to guide, support and mentor your progress and development. **More bluntly, find a speaking mentor or coach.**

Find someone who can help you advance to the next level. This person must be someone who is a successful speaker and understands the business. I would caution you on hiring a business coach who isn't in the speaking industry.

Whether you ask me to be your speaking mentor or you have someone else in mind, make a commitment to find someone. Your first $5,000+ speaking gig might depend on it. Often when someone agrees to mentor or coach you, they also make connections for you and help you grow your speaking network.

On the final page of this book, I have outlined what my coaching program looks like. My program is personalized 1-on-1 coaching and it breaks down this 5-module book in a 10-week program. I guide you along the way and answer questions each week to ensure the content is understandable and applied for your speaking goals and niche. There's many more features and benefits to the program so review the last page of this book for more details.

List below those people, or person, who could be your speaking mentor:

Now send them an email. Tell them they are important to you and that you respect and appreciate their mentorship to help you achieve your speaking goals.

You CAN do it. You WILL do it.
Do NOT quit 2 feet from gold.

Module Review

In this module, we have anchored principles to help you be successful as a PAID, professional speaker. We discussed

- the importance of developing and applying your system consistently,
- forecasting tough times so they are not a surprise,

- **identifying how hungry you are,**
- **surrounding yourself with support,**
- **showing appreciation and keeping in touch with your clients,**
- **both giving and getting referrals,**
- **finding a speaking mentor and, finally,**
- **setting realistic expectations.**

Congratulations! You have done it! I hope you feel not only inspired but also equipped with new knowledge that will support your journey to inspire others. You are embarking on one of the noblest of professions. Be authentic. Share your story. Be unique. Work harder than anyone else. Work smart. Inspire.

MODULE 5 CHECKLIST

	YES	**NO**
I understand the power of applying a consistent system.	____	____
I expect certain times to be tough as a speaker.	____	____
I am extremely hungry to become a successful speaker.	____	____
I plan to surround myself with support.	____	____
I have identified those people who will and will not understand my speaking aspirations.	____	____
I have a plan to show appreciation to clients.	____	____
I have a plan and system for keeping in touch.	____	____
I plan to give referrals for other speakers.	____	____
I will find at least one speaking mentor.	____	____
I plan to set realistic speaking expectations.	____	____

If you have checked 'YES' on all the items, CONGRATULATIONS! You have earned your thirty (30) minute coaching call to process this information!

NOTES

_____
_____
_____
_____

NOTES

NOTES

I WANT TO HEAR FROM YOU!

I would be honored to have your feedback as a **customer review on Amazon**. In appreciation for leaving a review, I will send you a complimentary copy of my best-selling eBook titled, "*Think Differently To Achieve Success!*"

I am also happy to provide you with that complimentary 30-minute coaching call to answer any questions you may have about the book and provide further explanation. Here's how you complete the Amazon review.

Simply follow these steps below:

#**1**: Visit www.Amazon.com

#**2**: In the Amazon search bar, type "How to Become a Professional Speaker and Kevin Snyder" so that you find the book online. Be sure to click on this book title!

#**3**: Then scroll down where it states "Write a Customer Review." Click that button. You will write your review here!

#**4**: After writing your review, send me an email at Kevin@KevinCSnyder.com. I will reply with your complimentary eBook and a scheduling link for your complimentary coaching call.

Note: Although Amazon.com preferred, you can also visit my website to make book reviews/purchases or contact me directly for bulk discount orders. (www.KevinCSnyder.com Kevin@KevinCSnyder.com)

To redeem your complimentary 30-minute coaching call, simply send an email to Kevin@KevinCSnyder.com. In the subject line, enter 'PAID to SPEAK Call.' In your message, provide at least three times during the following two weeks you are available for your coaching call. Someone will reply to schedule your phone conversation and provide you with more information pertaining to the call. If you have any questions in advance for the phone conversation, please include them in your message.

Important: This coaching call is only offered to those who have read and completed the questions in the book. Be sure to have your book available during the call.

What questions do you still have about becoming a speaker? List below questions and/or content that was not covered in the book:

About Dr. Kevin Snyder

Dr. Kevin Snyder is a motivational speaker and author with a passion for helping individuals take action to lead successful lives and achieve their fullest potential. He has spoken for over 1,000 audiences in all 50 U.S. states and over a dozen countries, has authored/co-authored over a dozen books and has recorded two instrumental piano CD's. He is also a former staff member aboard Semester at Sea, a certified skydiver and scuba diver, a sailing enthusiast, and winner on the game show 'The Price is Right!'

Kevin has also served as an adjunct faculty member with the Center for Creative Leadership (CCL) which is the global leader in executive education and training. His speakers bureau, Inspir-ACTIVE Solutions, specializes in developing custom-based keynotes and leadership development seminars to ignite employee motivation, satisfaction, workforce performance and enhanced bottom-line results. If your company or association ever seeks a dynamic keynote speaker, then consider Inspir-Active Solutions!

Kevin earned his Doctorate in Educational Leadership from the University of Central Florida, a Masters in Educational Administration from the University of South Carolina and a Bachelors in Marine Biology from the University of North Carolina at Wilmington. Contact him at:

www.KevinCSnyder.com   Kevin@KevinCSnyder.com

Connect with me on your 'social' of choice!

@KevinCSnyder

Download my app on your phone/iPad to get your "Daily Dose" of motivation, my free eBooks, leadership resources … & much more! Simply go to your app store and find KevinCSnyder

BONUS!

How to WRITE & FINISH Your Book in 90 Days!

Until now, writing a book required years and dozens - if not hundreds - of request letters to publishers to even get a response. Today with new publishing technologies and our experience helping hundreds of aspiring writers just like you, we can help you write your manuscript quicker than you ever thought possible! In just a short period of time, in as little as 90 days (3 months), we're confident we can help you FINISH and become an author! You're already taking the first step by reading this!

The only way to finish writing a book is to start the process. This may seem to be a simplistic statement, but it requires focus, discipline and accountability. Most aspiring authors struggle with knowing where to start on their book and how to condition their mind to be ready to write. As a result, writing becomes a chore, the writer themselves becomes frustrated, and the manuscript never gets finished.

In the next few pages, we'll help you get your mind ready to write. We'll outline our proven process with writers we've published that help you condition your mind "write," become more efficient when writing, organize the best outline possible, and end up with a completed manuscript in as little as 90 days ... or less! If you have the desire to become a published author, follow these clear action steps to make that desire a tangible reality!

Following each section, we'll be asking you a question or two that will help clarify and personalize this content for your book. Trust our process. Feedback from dozens of writers proves our recommendations are guidance are essential. Don't speed through these steps. We encourage you to think about and complete each question. You'll be conditioning yourself and focusing your mind so you can write in the "write" way!

But First ... What Constitutes A Book?

Today we can no longer think of a book as just bound printed pages. In addition to printed books, we also have digital books to read on eBook reader devices and audio books to listen. New technology has made it possible that books can now be enjoyed, and purchased, *in a variety of formats*.

These new technologies have also opened the door to new publishing opportunities, resulting in "gatekeeper" changes in the book world. Writers are no longer dependent on the big publishing houses to get their books published. Now authors can retain ownership and control of their work, publish them independently in the profitable new world of self-publishing, and retain well-deserved royalties.

Both the concept of what constitutes a book and the path that book takes to become published have changed irrevocably. Now the author, i.e. you (!), gets to decide what to deliver, when to deliver it, and in what form. This is an extraordinary new era for aspiring authors!

Books come in many genres, styles, formats, and lengths. Nonfiction, fiction, memoirs, family history, poetry, business, professional workbooks, self-help, cookbooks, collections of blog articles, a narrated speech, and children's books name a few broad genres. There is an audience, large or small, for any subject or book category you can envision.

The length of a book can be 30 pages, 300+ pages, or anything in between. People once assumed a "real" book could only be a thick novel or a lengthy non-fiction biography involving years of extensive research meeting "industry standard" approval from a publisher. These are <u>incorrect assumptions in today's book world</u> – which is why we formed Write Way Publishing Company! How else would aspiring authors know that publishing has never been more possible?

Your future book can be on any topic you wish, written in any length, and in your preferred style. Your book will be whatever *you* want it to be. You can have your book available globally on Amazon.com, or you can print only a few copies for family and friends. Because of technology, our society has evolved into a *do-it-yourself* era today, rich with experience and sharing opportunities that allow more people than ever before to learn from others. Do not convince yourself that you are not worthy to be an author. You are worthy because you have a message to share. Feel worthy to write!

Your intellectual property is your book. What you know is your book. Your business is your book. Your workshop or keynote presentation is your book. The story behind your achievements is your book. The story of your tragedy and struggle is your book. Whatever message you feel passionate about is your book!

Writing a book is about the desire to share your story, adventures, struggles, lessons, and what you have learned through research or experience. It can be any length or belong to any genre. Share what you know. Share what inspires *you* so that you can be an inspiration to *others*. There have never been more resources available to help you become published than there are "write" now. Doesn't this feel incredible to read?

Now that we have primed your mind to know that holding your book is just a matter of time, are you ready to start? Keep reading!

START HERE BEFORE YOU BEGIN!

Know Your Purpose For Writing

Knowing your "why" for writing your book and anchoring this reason, or reasons, will help you persist and complete the book-writing marathon. There will be times of frustration and times of writer's block, times of doubt and times of feeling "over it."

It's during these times that you must press on, reminding yourself why you are writing, and, of course, thinking about the benefits you will receive once you become a published author. The work you do now will have a multi-fold positive impact on your future, your family, and your finances!

So what is your "why"? Is it for personal fulfillment, to build personal/business credibility, to generate additional income for your business, to leave a legacy, to inspire others, to share your hard earned knowledge? Knowing your *"why,"* your purpose in writing, will help get you out of bed at 4:00 a.m. or put you in your writing space at midnight when the house gets quiet and you need the discipline to write without distractions.

Write below your "why" for writing your book. Why is it important to you?

Getting Your Mind "Write"

Getting your mind "write" so it is ready to write is an imperative first step to the successful completion of your book manuscript. Focus on writing your manuscript and nothing else. Don't think about your book layout, font style, editing, cover, publishing, or book sales at this point. That is important but it will come later. Focus on only writing the manuscript draft. You have nothing to edit, publish, or sell if the manuscript is not complete first.

But where to start? How do you determine your content? How do you organize your material? How do you avoid distractions? What will happen if you get writer's block? At what point should you start editing? And the very real issue—how do you find time to write in your already crowded schedule?

The only way you can begin writing your book is by first getting your mind focused and staying disciplined to a writing system that works for you. Get your mind "write" first and foremost! Don't start writing before you are ready. Don't FIRE, AIM, and then get READY! Instead, get READY, AIM ... and then WRITE! Follow our system.

The main components of our recommended system to help you get your mind "write" and ready are:

- **Know when you're most alert**
- **Schedule regular blocks of time to write without distractions**
- **Expect frustrations**
- **Be realistic with expectations**

High-quality book content is essential to your book's success, but it is the "**system**" you apply that will allow you to create your content and write your book manuscript. Not following a system is a guarantee to eventually feeling frustrated, hitting writer's block, and getting overwhelmed. Commit to yourself that you identify your system so that you write efficiently and enjoy the process!

In the next few pages, we'll explain more about how to understand our system so that you can customize your own and finish your manuscript quickly. It all starts with getting your mind ready to write. Let's get ready!

Getting READY, Step 1: Know When You Are Most Alert

When are you most alert? Are you an early morning person or a night person? Are you at your prime early morning while your spouse is still asleep and the world is still waking up, or are you at your best late afternoon over a cup of coffee? Also, due to your work and life schedule, when can you reliably set aside time to write during your most alert period? What schedule and writing timeframe is best for you?

When you discover your time of day and environment that helps you find maximum focus, clear of distractions, for several hours, that is the time for you to write. Don't write early in the morning if you're not a morning person. Don't write in the late evening if you routinely get tired after a full day of work and family activities. If you have a full-time job, then perhaps you only have the time and energy to schedule writing time on weekends.

Most people don't know when they are at their optimum so you may have to experiment a little to figure this out. The point is, know when your mind is most alert so that you can write the "Write Way!"

When is your best time to write? Describe when are you at your optimum?

***Getting READY, Step 2**: Schedule Time Without Distractions*

You no doubt schedule time for important things you want to accomplish, so why not schedule time to write? If writing a book is a significant goal for you, then you need to make time to do it. Tell those who are important to you that you are embarking on writing a book that will require focus and dedication, and that you likely will not be as available to them as you normally are for a few weeks.

Many things we want to accomplish require some sacrifice. Becoming an author is no exception. If writing a book were easy, everyone would be doing it. It's hard, and it's time-consuming to become an author. That's why most people don't achieve the status of "author." It's tough and requires considerable determination and focus.

We frequently hear from aspiring authors that they try to fit writing into their schedule, rather than scheduling their time to write. We have *never* worked with someone who finished their manuscript by writing 15-30 minutes a day. On the contrary, we've worked with many people who broke through the struggles and frustration until by realizing they simply had to hold themselves accountable to scheduling time to write. It is this simple!

It is crucial that you schedule your time to write. Tell everyone—your family, friends and even your boss—that you are making time to write a book, and that soon you will be a published author! Remember, it's only a short period of time and then you will have your book forever. Keep the end in mind.

Setting aside time and keeping to your writing schedule will help you stay motivated because you will see regular, real progress toward finishing your book. Firmly keeping your dedicated writing time intact will let your mind look forward to and prepare for the next writing session. A schedule you abide by will minimize the temptation to let other things distract you and pull you away from your writing.

Look at your schedule and prioritize your time. Find two to three-hour blocks of time at least twice a week to work on your book plus a four-hour block on weekends. Scheduling blocks of time to write will give you time to settle into your writing zone each session and will give you a very do-able eight to ten hours a week of writing time. Yes, this may mean giving up some leisure time, or time with family and friends, or some other time sacrifice, but remember, this is only temporary, and there is a reward at the end—your book!

When it's time to write, treat the time with respect. Turn off your phone, close down your social media and email, and put yourself in an environment where you will not be distracted. Let's think about that environment for a moment. Depending on your schedule and your preferences, you may prefer to find a quiet place at home to write, or you may prefer to go to a local café, coffee shop, or some other place of inspiration to work. The important thing is to find a place where you can get your writing done.

It usually takes 15-20 minutes just to get relaxed and mentally zoned in at the beginning of each writing period. Choose to have things around you to make you comfortable and relaxed. Music or no music, solitude or bustling coffee shop, favorite beverage handy, writing supplies at the ready. Often building a routine around your writing time will help you hit your writing zone more quickly and easily.

If you don't feel focused and zoned in, it's likely because you haven't scheduled time to be distraction free, or you haven't placed yourself in the "write" environment.

<u>Describe the best place and environment for you to write.</u>

<u>Write the days and times during a week that you can schedule writing time.</u>

Now put these days and times on your calendar!
In addition to scheduling undistracted, specific times to write, you must hold yourself accountable for getting your work from your head onto a page. There's no point in scheduling time on the calendar if you're not going to

follow through. For your book to get written within some reasonable timeframe, you must make and keep writing time a priority. One of the biggest reasons why writers don't become published authors is they do not commit to getting their writing done.

In our writer workshops, students are asked to evaluate what was most helpful in the course. Overwhelmingly they have replied, "accountability"! Of course, you're not going to get a weekly grade on your book's progress, but there are other ways you can use accountability to stay on course.

Post on social media that you're writing a book and share the anticipated publication date or some other significant deadline. Let co-workers know, and they will very likely ask you about your progress.

We encourage you to find someone in your circle who would be willing to check in with you once or twice a month or make time for you to call them periodically with a progress report. These reports do not have to be long conversations, but they should report on real work accomplished or discuss a stumbling block you encountered and what you're doing about it.
When you keep an eye on your calendar timeline and know someone is going to expect an update from you, you'll be amazed at how much more productive you'll be! We provide author coaching and writer accountability as well.

Contact us if this staying on track and accountable to your weekly/monthly writing goals is an issue you have been struggling. We understand!

Who is someone who can serve as your accountability partner?

Getting READY, Step 3: Expect Frustrations

We venture to say every author experiences frustrations while writing their book. They have encountered a moment, or even days, when they felt frustrated or mentally exhausted.

As long as writers expect these moments, they won't be caught off guard. Frustrations can occur anytime, especially during the initial outline generation phase, through edits and re-edits, when writer's block sets in, or even with something as simple as getting stuck on a particular word or concept.

Accept that frustrations will come. The question is how do you get your *mojo*, focus, or energy back? During times of frustration you just need to take a break. Here are some things to try:

- Go for a walk
- Grab a drink or snack
- Talk with someone close to you about what is happening
- Meditate or perform breathing exercises
- Re-read your previous chapter to get the flow back
- Look at your outline and think about what you will work on next
- Work on a different part of your manuscript

If you don't actively deal with the frustration, you'll become frustrated by the simple fact you're frustrated! *Expect frustrations.* It's part of the writing journey and something every author must break through.

<u>What are frustrations you foresee when writing</u>?

Why do you feel you are experiencing, or might experience, those frustrations?

Getting READY, Step 4: Be Realistic With Expectations

You probably want that book published *yesterday*. Writing is one more thing calling for your time and energy in an already busy schedule. You're investing part of your life in writing your book, sacrificing other significant priorities to achieve it. When finishing the book seems overwhelming, take a few minutes to savor the anticipation of having your book completed. Imagine holding a copy of your very own book in your hand. Envision it in someone else's hand too! You can manifest this vision by staying focused and disciplined in the writing process. Sometimes you will just need to remind yourself that you **will** be a published author soon.

Your Calendar. We've talked about the power of a three-month calendar, but, of course, that time length will vary depending on each writing project. The principles of creating the calendar will stay the same no matter the period covered. What does that calendar timeline look like for you? If you're planning an opus with the scope of *War and Peace,* obviously you will need more than three months writing time. You need at least some idea of the scope of your book. Is it 60-90 pages or 250+? Now ask yourself when you'd like to have the first draft complete. Be realistic.

<u>Write down the specific date you realistically think the first draft of your manuscript will be written</u>.

Now circle this date, smile, and congratulate yourself!
It's on this date that all your work will be worth the investment you've made!
Begin and write with the end in mind!

Now that you have committed to that important date work backward on your calendar and mark off as many two or three-hour writing time blocks as you realistically can afford. Be clear about your expectations for when your book will be finished. Assess the time in your schedule you think you can set aside to write. Does the available time seem realistic to achieving your manuscript draft date? If not, will you add more writing time or move back the first draft date?

With the realistic first draft target date in mind, chunk your writing process in segments. Here are some very general tasks to consider using a non-fiction book draft on a familiar topic to be completed in 90-days as an example:

- Write a brief (2-3 sentence) paragraph summarizing the concept for your book.
- List ideas you want to cover in your book.
- Devise a content outline based on the topics.
- Create chapter divisions.
- Set weekly word/page writing goals. The actual word count will vary based on good writing days and slow writing days, but the numbers will give you

targets and keep you on track. Mark word or page goals on your calendar. For example, you could write about 5000 words a month for three months to create a 60-page book. Assuming an average of 250 words a page, this means writing only about 20 pages a month. Divide this out based on the number of your writing periods in the month to set word or page goals for each writing session. Fewer writing periods, more words/pages per period! Don't obsess about the goal numbers, but do try to stay on track.

- Mark your accountability report dates.

Have you heard the saying that the only way to eat an elephant is one bite at a time? Apply that lesson here and create a writing timetable that breaks writing tasks into manageable chunks that aren't overwhelming.

Now That You Are <u>READY</u> & Have Your Mind "Write," It's Time To <u>AIM</u>!

AIM, Step One: *Create Your Outline First*

When planning a journey to a specific destination, you need directions—a roadmap if you will. Likewise, in writing your book, you must know where you want to go and how to get there. Otherwise, you'll be driving around aimlessly.

A book outline is akin to a roadmap for writing your manuscript. It's important that you have a general sense of how you want your book to be organized. Without an outline, there's a tendency to meander, forget relevant issues, or get lost trying to make your key points.

You have gotten your mind "write" already, put considerable thought into your system for how you're going to write, and scheduled time accordingly. Begin your book manuscript by creating an outline for all the material you want to cover. Make this a fun process, and expect your outline to change and evolve.

Here's a good way to get your thoughts flowing. Start by writing down thoughts, themes, chapter title headings, subtitle headings—anything on topic that comes to mind. Write on a memo pad, on sticky notes, on a whiteboard, etc. What's most important is getting your thoughts written out. It will clear your mind and allow your creative juices to flow.

The more you can write down, the better. Don't censor. Don't edit. Don't put limits on your thoughts. Just write ideas that come to mind. You won't get everything in one swoop, but you will get a good start. As you work, more ideas will come to you. What we're describing to you is also called a brain dump.

Now you need to organize that jumble of ideas into an outline for your book. Identify and isolate your main topics as "travel" points on your road map. Then group and circle related ideas and patterns as subtopics under the topics. From there add bullets for key points you want to make under each subtopic.

Before you know it, you'll have a rough working outline pulled together. This process works especially well for non-fiction books. Using plot points within this process (instead of topic ideas) can help you create an outline for your fiction book.

Here's another way to think about this process … imagine you are putting a 1,000-piece puzzle together. What do you do first?

Most people, place the lid of the puzzle box in front of them and then dump all the pieces out on the table. After scanning the pieces, they begin sorting through puzzle pieces pairing common colors, edge shapes, and patterns. Another approach that helped many of our clients successfully develop their outline is allocating a wall for sticky notes. Each sticky note is a "puzzle piece" of content that you feel could be in your book. Whether it's a story, a quote, a lesson, a metaphor, an experience, etc. – write only one per sticky note. As you write these sticky notes, place them onto a clean wall or whiteboard.

Tip: you'll need more space than you think so use an entire wall or get a very large whiteboard! And remember, there are no limits to this process. Just because you write down a thought doesn't mean you have to use it.

Once you have "brain dumped" all the ideas you could possibly have, take a step back and look at your wall. Appreciate and relish all your ideas. You'll likely be very surprised how much content you have! Because your ideas are all written down and you can actually see your book unfolding, you'll feel progress. You'll also be flooded with more clarity than you've ever had before. This will make more sense once you do it. Trust the process.

Now ask someone who knows you well and is aware you are writing a book, i.e. your spouse or a close friend, to come look at your outline wall. Have them scan your ideas and ask them to share any thoughts you may have overlooked. Since they know you well, they likely have additional stories, memories and experiences you can consider including.

As additional ideas come to you throughout this entire process, remember that you can add sticky notes anytime you wish. You will likely also decide not to include certain sticky notes, but do not throw them away! Rather, move them into a "parking lot" area of your wall or whiteboard. You might decide to use them later or perhaps even in your second book! You initially wrote them down for a reason.

Once you feel you have posted sufficient amounts of sticky notes, start looking for common patterns, themes and categories. Begin grouping these common sticky note themes together in hopes of identifying a content flow. Treat your outline generation just like putting a puzzle together. It'll likely take a few sittings to complete, but piece by piece, your outline will begin to take shape.

After you have categories grouped, then decide the order of categories to be introduced in your book. Nothing is set in stone and things can be moved as needed. What's most important during this outline generation phase is to get ideas out so your mind becomes more clear and that you have a roadmap to write!

Step 1: Brain Dump

Step 2: Look for common themes

Step 3: Organize and categorize

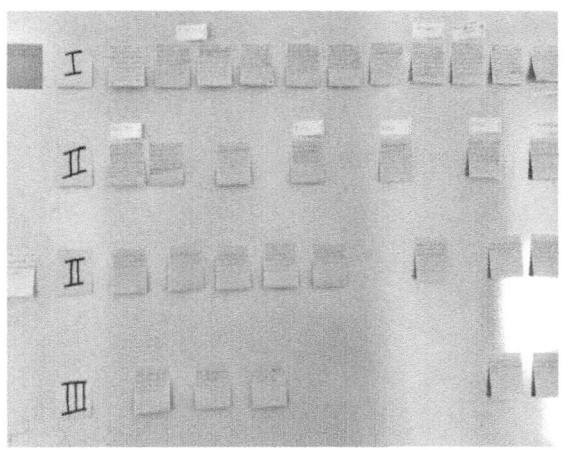

Step 4: Decide order to write

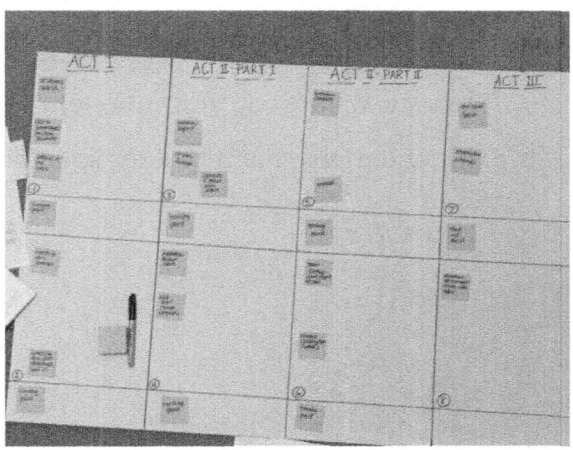

Creating your outline is not that difficult but it requires time and focus. It also requires a system to identify your content and some time to organize. Even after you begin writing, you are likely going to make modifications to your outline. As any changes are made, be sure to keep your revised outline updated.

Tip: Be prepared for ideas to enter your mind at unexpected times. Do not risk losing those "aha" moments and precious content opportunities by saying yourself, "I'll remember that." Unfortunately, you likely won't and that great idea is unfortunately forever gone.

Expect "aha" moments at completely random times and in unexpected environments. Keep a notebook or recording device on you at all times and especially where you spend large amounts of time—in your office, your car, your home office, your bathroom, even beside your bed. Carry a voice recorder on your next long drive or walk. Place a dry erase board in your shower. Carry a small notepad and pen with you through the day or be ready to record notes on your phone. Text yourself ideas. Write yourself emails and file them in an email folder specifically for your book ideas.

<u>Invest 15 minutes right now and begin making a list of points you plan to include in your book. Write them below.</u>

Congratulations! If the preceding page is full of ideas, you're well on your way! This list is just a start for your outline, but it's a good one. If you have questions or get stuck, let us know. We love helping develop book outlines.

Ready. Aim.

AIM, Step 2: **The Power of the Dedication**

The book dedication is a powerful inspiration for persisting in writing to book completion. By writing the dedication, you know you are writing in honor of someone or something important to you. After you write your outline, or perhaps even before, write your dedication and put it somewhere visible, so you see it every time you write. Post it on your wall or tape it to your computer. Looking at it will inspire you to do your best and to persevere when you get stuck because want to deliver on your dedication!

Write your book dedication below.

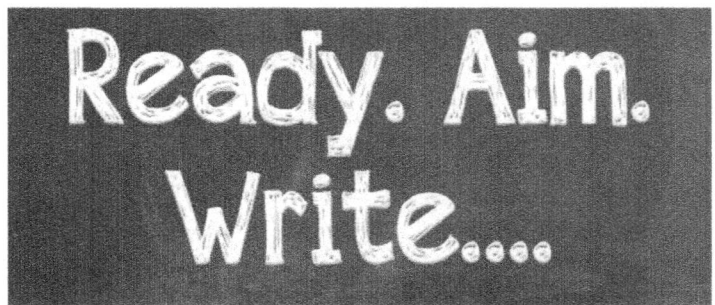

WRITE, Step One: *Writing Your Manuscript*

You have your writing calendar laid out, your writing time is scheduled, your "why" is anchored, your mind is ready, those people important to you understand you'll be writing often, your outline in front of you, and your dedication posted for inspiration … now it's time to write!

Use your outline with its topics, subtopics, and bullet points, and begin to develop the ideas you want to share.

Do not for a single minute think you will write from the first word to the last in smooth and final progression. You may find yourself jumping from chapter 3 to chapter 10, or moving chapter 4 to chapter 2. You may eventually rewrite the better part of an entire chapter (not the same as editing!) as your book develops. These kinds of things are part of the creative process. Allow your inspiration the opportunity to guide you.

The important thing is that you are *writing* your book! Stay with your system. Pay attention to your schedule. Don't get bogged down or frustrated with yourself. If one part isn't flowing, move to a different section or chapter, and come back later to the problem area.

The important success principle we can share with you is to keep to your system. Keep this document handy down the road so that when you do encounter any issues or challenges, you can review this document to remind yourself it's OK! We've never worked with a writer who didn't experience some sort of frustration or setback along the way.

When you do experience any issues, contact us! We'll talk you through it. We can help you finish the mountain of manuscript writing --- Mount Manuscript! Writing the manuscript is such a significant portion of the entire book writing experience. Remind yourself that once it's done, it's DONE! You will then have the majority of your future book complete.

After the Manuscript is Complete ... What's Next?

Editing is a must. You should not format or have your manuscript uploaded until a professional editor has reviewed your manuscript. Otherwise, you'll be making changes and it will become extremely expensive and labor intensive.

Editing cannot occur until the manuscript is complete. Editing is important because it provides another set of careful eyes on your work. While you should always consider the source of the feedback, having an editor, or editors, for your writing will provide you with needed perspective. Editors will see issues that you will not, including errors and phrasing that need clarification.

Should you hire an editor? Absolutely. You should find someone who does editing professionally and has edited before. A friend who enjoys reading is not an editor. A beta reader is not an editor. Even someone who claims to be an editor may not actually be a professional editor. An editor needs to be someone who you trust to review your manuscript with the utmost professionalism and experience.

You do not want a misspelled word in your book or a phrase that just doesn't make sense. Since you've read, and re-read, your book many times, you might be blind to text corrections that need to be made. An editor with a fresh perspective and lens will catch needed edits you'll likely miss. It is imperative that you have your manuscript edited before you format and upload it for a printed proof copy.

There are several different kinds of editing. For now, we will just mention copyediting and proofreading. A copy editor will read your manuscript, line by line, for text errors, confusing passages, continuity, incorrectly used words, and the like. Often this requires more than one pass through the manuscript. It is up to you whether you accept or reject any edit. Be sure to keep an open mind!

Once you have revised your work to your satisfaction and created a clean copy, then a proof editor takes over to search out misspelled words, errant commas, added spaces, poor sentence breaks—all those annoying little things that can make your book look less than professionally done.

The challenge becomes finding the right person or persons to serve as your editor(s). Again, for best editing results, choose editors who are not friends or family. Choose people who can provide the level of editing services you need. In many of our publishing packages, we include editing! Visit our website for more details.

Select an editor carefully and choose someone who is familiar with your book genre. A business book editor might not be the best choice for the romance novel or memoir you're writing!

Have questions about editing? Contact us by visiting our website - WriteWayPublishingCompany.com.

<u>List names of people or resources who can provide editing support for your manuscript</u>. (*Remember, we can help as well!*)

What About Interior Layout and Formatting?

In what format should your book be written? How should the book be laid out? What font type and size should you use? What about margins? What resolution is necessary for pictures or images, and how should they be submitted? What about color preferences and type of paper?

These are all great and important questions. There are many more considerations you should be making as well! However, if you are just beginning to write your book, do not even think about these questions just yet. Focus only on your writing and finishing your manuscript.

A book not properly formatted will never be approved for publishing! Furthermore, it will end up costing you considerable extra time and cost. We have created an "Interior Layout Tip Sheet" and would be happy to send this to you. Simply contact us and we will be happy to send you our resource that we share with our authors.

Unless you are experienced with layout and formatting, let your publisher handle this for you. Formatting requires professional design expertise. Do not spend needless hours trying to format your book yourself. You need to know formatting specifications and how to properly set up your book for the printer who is publishing your book.

What About Cover Design?

Your cover is the first impression others will have of your book. It will also be the deciding factor whether people will purchase your book or not.

Similar to editing and interior formatting, designing a book cover requires professional design expertise. It also requires knowledge on setting up the cover file so that your publisher can approve and print the cover successfully.

We've worked with many writers who attempted to design their own cover, or had a friend design their cover for them. Unfortunately, the amount of time it required to make corrections and adjustments ended up costing more than if we had just designed the cover for them to begin with. A book cover not properly designed will never be approved for publishing.

We have created an "Book Cover Design Tip Sheet" and would be happy to send this to you. Simply contact us and we will be happy to send you our resource that we share with our authors. Unless you are experienced with cover design, let your publisher handle this for you. Again though, if you are just beginning to write your book, do not even think about these questions just yet. Focus only on your writing and finishing your manuscript.

How To Find a Publisher?

Write Way Publishing Company works with writers in any location, any genre, and all types of books. Our team prides itself on over-delivering and providing the best value for your investment. Our philosophy is that our book is as important to us as it is to you.

Our founders have published books themselves so we understand every detail that is required to publish a book successfully. Our one-stop-approach approach ensures no detail is left out. Anything a writer needs to successfully write, publish, and promote their book is a service we can provide.

Contact us so we can talk more about your book and learn more about you. Our consultations are free and we can offer you a variety of free resources. We also provide editorial assessments on work you have already written. Assessments are a great start to help you write on track and finish!

Final Thoughts

Are you feeling clear on where to start? Are you feeling more confident in your direction and ability to write your book? We hope so! Reading this far proves you are serious about writing and becoming a published author. We would love to hear from you and will happily provide a complimentary consultation. We are passionate about all kinds of book genres and, humbly, we're pretty good at getting our aspiring authors to the publishing stage!

Before we close this chapter so you can begin writing *yours*, let's recap 12 important concepts you have learned:

- *The only person who can write your book is ... you!*
- *Current technology has given an exciting new definition for "published author."*
- *Knowing your "why," your purpose for writing, is a powerful motivator.*
- *It's important to get your mind "write" before you start writing.*
- *Identifying and working within your alert times*
- *Scheduling time to write fosters focus and helps you meet your writing goals.*
- *Having an accountability partner will help you stay on track.*
- *Expecting frustrations along the way and dealing with them before they get out of hand will make your writing path smoother.*
- *Developing your book outline provides you with a roadmap for writing.*
- *Your book dedication can provide you with powerful inspiration and motivation to get your book completed.*
- *Editing is an essential part of the writing process, but write first, edit later!*
- *Write Way Publishing Company is here to help you! Contact us for a complimentary consultation and learn more!*

We hope you will put what you've learned here to work to get your book written. It's not easy, but it's do-able if you make your writing a priority. Write the book once and benefit long term for all the reasons you wanted to write your book!

A Special Offer for you ...

How incredible would it feel to have your manuscript written in 90 days or less? Would it be beneficial for you to have support and guidance while you're writing? How exciting would it be to write alongside other aspiring authors just like you in a 90-day program to get your book draft completed?

We've developed the "Write Your Book in 90 Days" program to offer those benefits and more! We truly want you to become a published author. It's your time**! Our 3-month program is designed to support, guide, and coach you to have a manuscript ready in 3-months!** Check out these details below:

"Write a Book in 90 Days"

- Access to all WWPC Guides / Library
- Monthly intensive workshop
- Personalized coaching
- Group mentoring calls/webinars
- Sample proof edit (1,500 words)
- Peer reviews of your work
- Private Facebook group
- Audio / eBook conversion support

TOTAL VALUE $2,770+

... and more!

The [program is offered at] a special price. Since we run special discounts for certain types of groups and writers, simply inquire with us for details on when our next class is being scheduled and special pricing.

These classes will be small enough for personal attention but big enough to enjoy peer support and review! The course will only be offered 3 times a year.

If you feel that coaching, support, guidance, and peer support along the way would be helpful for you to get your book written, contact us today! Send a message to Info@WriteWayPublishingCompany.com or just write **"90 Day Book Course"** in the last box in our contact form! (If you want to share a little information about your writing project, fill out as little or as much as you want in this form.)

TO YOUR SPEAKING AND PUBLISHING SUCCESS!

Dr. Kevin C. Snyder

PAID TO SPEAK IN 10 WEEKS – COACHING PROGRAM

There seem to be many coaches for speakers. Make sure you work with one who actually speaks professionally, understands what it takes, has spoken over 1,000 times, and will personalize a program just for you!

IN JUST 10 WEEKS, MY SPEAKER COACHING PROGRAM WILL TEACH YOU:
- … how to become a successful professional speaker in a proven, updated 5-module system with workbook!
- … how to design a powerfully engaging keynote guaranteed to demand referrals where they call you!
- … how to create proposals, contracts and invoices that will double your fees!
- … how to avoid common speaker pitfalls, myths, and frustrations that force most speakers to quit!
- … how to write and publish a book in as little as 90 days - eBook and audiobook too!
- … how to leverage your book to make thousands more each speaking gig!
- … and so much more!

ELEMENTS OF THE PROGRAM INCLUDE:
- PAID to SPEAK workbook sharing 15 years of experience.
- 10 weeks of personalized coaching. No lame recordings.
- My personal review with feedback of <u>all</u> your material.
- Group coaching phone/web conferences.
- Sample copies of everything needed as a speaker:
  (i.e. presentations, proposals, and contracts)
- Exclusive Facebook group with other speakers.
- I will help you identify at least 10 target groups who pay!
- You'll receive a "Daily speaker tip" text directly from me.
- Full access to me … ask anything you want. No holds barred.
- <u>NEW</u>! Along with other speakers building their business like you, we'll close with a sailing retreat excursion.
- Author coaching & resources to write and publish your book!

My personal guarantee is that you will develop a clear plan for exactly where to start in achieving your speaking goals. I'll work beside you along the way for 10 full weeks. I'll share everything I have and review everything you share!

READY TO GET STARTED?

Kevin@KevinCSnyder.com
#919-633-9931
www.KevinCSnyder.com

PAID To $PEAK!™: How to Become a Professional Speaker www.PAIDToSPEAK.biz   www.KevinCSnyder.com

Made in the USA
Monee, IL
02 December 2019

17777818R00142